Leonard Low was born in F
Upper Largo. He moved to
work on building sets for film.
colour-blind, his paintings are much sought after. He has
two children and a giant ginger cat called Hamish. A long-
standing fascination with the dark side of history resulted in
his first book, *The Weem Witch*. Lenny has a house in Lundin
Links and still has a passion for East Fife FC, but admits that
they do not always live up to his high expectations.

By the same author

The Weem Witch
There Are Such Things!

LARGO'S UNTOLD STORIES

LEONARD LOW

Best Wishes

Steve Savage
LONDON AND EDINBURGH

Steve Savage Publishers Ltd
The Old Truman Brewery
91 Brick Lane
LONDON
E1 6QL

www.savagepublishers.com

First published in Great Britain by Steve Savage Publishers Ltd 2013

Copyright © Leonard Low 2013

ISBN: 978-1-904246-39-8

Typeset by Steve Savage Publishers
Printed and bound by SRP Ltd, Exeter

MIX
Paper from
responsible sources
FSC® C014540

Contents

Acknowledgements   p7

Picture Credits   p9

Chapters

1 – Bones   p11

2 – The Largo Picts Fight Roman Occupation   p36

3 – The Pirate Sir Andrew Wood   p48

4 – Witches   p64

5 – Lamont's Diary   p73

6 – What Shall We Do with a Drunken Sailor?   p96

7 – The Madness of Andrew Mason   p115

8 – Not So Good Sir!   p132

9 – Today's Largo   p152

Sources   p156

This book is dedicated to John Wotton
of Crouch End, London.
A very very funny man taken by a horrid
wasting disease in September 2012,
my love to his family.

Acknowledgements

This is the third book I have written, and my most personal book to date. Largo is where I was born and now live. I have had these stories beside me all my life and cannot fathom why no one has written about them all before, putting them in one volume. For such a small place, the information contained in these stories is startling. There are no obvious monuments or plaques for the tourist to follow. The one exception is Alexander Selkirk (Robinson Crusoe), who probably deserves a statue least out of all the characters I have covered in this book.

As with my previous books *The Weem Witch* and *There Are Such Things*, I have a small army of helpers I would be hopeless without. I am a one-finger typewriter user: I need fourteen-year-old nerds to help me download photos I've taken. When the laptop stops working, you would be better off advising my cat Hamish how to solve the problem rather than telling me.

I would like to thank the illustrious Ian Muirhead, Bruce Marshall, Stephen Gilfeather and his lovely trio of daughters, John Van Dieken, William McLean, David Low for the Ptolemy map, Donald Low for information on Captain Mason's ship and the photo of Vatersay, Linda Whiteford and Margo, Jamie Rowbotham, John the Bet,

Irish Jocky and my old pal, never far from my thoughts but a continent away, Ian Pirie.

Not forgetting my two children, Callum and Kirsty Low.

My love to Ruth, a whirlwind of love and laughter.

Great thanks of a humongous kind to David Baxter for sending me newspaper articles that appear about my projects. I would never have known about them, because I was in London. Lots of newspapers steal from other papers, and I am sometimes stunned to find myself featuring in a newspaper or magazine that hasn't even approached me! I am mostly clueless about what has been printed until David kindly buys it, sticks it in the letterbox of my house in Largo and lets me know.

Thanks to the *East Fife Mail*, especially Scott Inglis for his enthusiasm and patience, the *Scottish Sun*, *Daily Record*, London's *Evening Standard*, Dundee's *The Courier*, *Islington Gazette*, *Ham and High*, *Crouch End Journal*, *Edinburgh Dungeons* and the *Fortean Times* magazine and the more than thirty other newspapers and magazines which have covered me in one way or another, from photos of ghosts at Archway Hospital to trying to raise a memorial to the Pittenweem witches.

To the tens of people who actually openly dislike the stones I turn over and the doors of history I open, to the hundreds of people who have come on my 'Weem Witch' tours in Pittenweem, to the thousands of readers who bought my first two books ... with a tear in my eye, I truly thank you all!

Leonard Low

London – soon to be Lundin Links

Picture Credits

Thank you to Moira Greig for allowing me to use material from the article she co-wrote with Colvin Greig and Patrick Ashmore, 'Excavation of a cairn cemetery at Lundin Links, Fife, in 1965-6', which appeared in *Proceedings of the Society of Antiquaries of Scotland* in 2000. I am grateful to the Society of Antiquaries of Scotland for permission to reproduce illustration 1 on p15, illustration 2 on p16, illustration 3 on p17, illustration 4 on p18, illustration 5 on p19 and illustration 7 on p26.

Illustrations 6 on pp24–25, by permission of Department of Anatomy, Dundee Museum

Illustration 18 on p126, Donald Low

Illustrations 19 on p139 and 21 on p149, by permission of The National Maritime Museum

Illustrations 20 on p147 and 21 on p148 are reprinted from *Journal of Archaeological Science*, vol 38, issue 7, S. Mays, A. Ogden, J. Montgomery, S. Vincent, W. Battersby, G. M. Taylor, 'New light on the personal identification of a skeleton of a member of Sir John Franklin's last expedition to the Arctic, 1845', pp1571–1582, copyright 2011, with permission from Elsevier.

Chapter 1

Bones

Largo Bay, with its horseshoe shape, has sand dunes around its circumference, with coarse grass behind. A light gradient leads us down the golden sandy beach stretching for a hundred yards or more in places. In the summer on a decent day you can actually think you're in a Mediterranean surrounding — until your toes dip into the first inch of the sea and your mind is instantly transported to the Baltic.

There are rocky outcrops here which are fantastic for crab hunters, and at low tide herons and seals can be seen to soak up the summer rays and steal a meal where available. It is a tranquil place, full of dog walkers, golfers practising their swing; brave swimmers in the summer months will come from afar to enjoy the water, and ramblers meander along the sands, walking off into the distance.

It is nature at its unspoilt best: gulls overhead cry and dive headlong into the sea, catching a few of the swarms of sand eels at the turn of the tide. Small armies of oystercatchers march up and down the sands at low tide digging in the sand for food. Littered all along the seafront are volcanic bombs, huge rounded stone deposits blown from an erupting Largo Law. The stones tell of its volcanic violence many millennia ago, ranging from cannonball size to ten tonnes in weight. Almost 290 metres high, the volcano is now extinct.

At sea, there is a small, shimmering fleet of yachts. They twist and turn, using their sails to gain a purchase on what wind is available. Occasionally in the sky a one-man microlight aircraft will fly overhead with the hum of an angry bee, navigating the air currents and eventually landing on the hard flat sands. In the distance across the water lies the May Island, a bird sanctuary now, but still sitting watching over the Firth of Forth with its little sister the Bass Rock, its cliffs white from centuries of gull guano.

Occasionally in winter months, after a storm, if the conditions are right, the sands in the bay can shift completely. Thousands of tonnes of sand will disappear overnight, and then the bare rock is exposed, revealing fantastic fossils — ferns, trees and small shells embedded into the prehistoric rock, laid naked by the migrating sand for a brief moment. Here interested local geologists find evidence that in the distant past, in the Jurassic era, the bay was once a forest. This exposure has to be admired and recorded quickly, for after a few full tides the sands will gradually return. In a matter of weeks the bay will regain its golden sheen.

It happened in 1965. The skies overhead darkened heavily, the winter storm came, the north wind blew, and waves smashed and tore at the beach in a terrible fury that lasted for days. Once the danger had passed and the storm had lost its power, it was noticed the golden sands had shifted; the black rock was laid bare. Fossils were showing once again. But this time the wild storm that displaced the sands exposed something else, something new — the bones of two feet!

The two feet were still attached to a skeleton, buried further into the sand.

The discovery, although quite a shock to those who made it, was not so very unusual; several bodies had been found and recorded near this area in 1856 and again in 1858 during the construction of the railway.

(The 1856 skeleton was found at what was then known as Johnston's Mill; when dug up by the workmen the bones actually fell to dust.)

Thirteen cists (stone graves) had been found during quarrying for the railway lines. Two were found while building the station itself and a further four were found before 1862. They were found about a metre underground; stone slabs in several layers, two or three to a side. The occupants of the cists were in good condition. One skeleton showed a skull penetration — a heavy head wound, possibly caused by a sword or spear, that would have resulted in his death.

The skeleton found on the beach in the 1960s, with its feet sticking out, was carefully excavated. After tests, it was found to be that of a woman, of 40 to 45 years of age, and about 150 centimetres in height. The disturbing thing about this find was that the skeleton was seated in an upright position, with three stone slabs over its legs, almost as if sitting down for dinner! Its arms were stretched out on each side at shoulder level. The entire remains were covered by coarse sand which had been heaped on top, with a ring of shells surrounding the bones.

This was no average person: the burial and preparation of the corpse showed a kindness only given to respected people. Although a primitive ceremony, the preparation involved suggested this was indeed a much loved person.

The evidence available to the archaeologists who descended on the area suggested a burial during the first millennium. A fragment of stone slab with a symbol scratched into the surface suggested a Pictish origin, but it was not clear, being rather weathered and worn. Further examination of the nearby area revealed a further two circular cairns behind the first. It was decided that the site needed some serious excavating by professionals. Over the Easter break in 1965, the Aberdeen College of Education Archaeological Society was called to undertake two weeks' serious study in the immediate area.

The dig got under way and further stone cists appeared a few metres north of the two stone cairns originally unearthed. Soon five more graves had been discovered by these two cairns and the original first skeleton. From the hip bones the scientists could determine that the skeletons all appeared to be of women interred in the graves. On further investigation, four more cairns appeared from the sand. It was evident that this was a burial ground of great significance.

Two central cairns now appeared, of contrasting appearance to the others, one in a figure-of-eight shape of 2 by 2.4 metres. It had an outside ring of stones surrounding the structure (like a concave igloo), and contained the skeleton of a male, possibly 40 to 50 years old and 178 centimetres in height. No grave goods were found, only a bedding of shells. The other cairn contained another male skeleton aged around 35 to 40. The

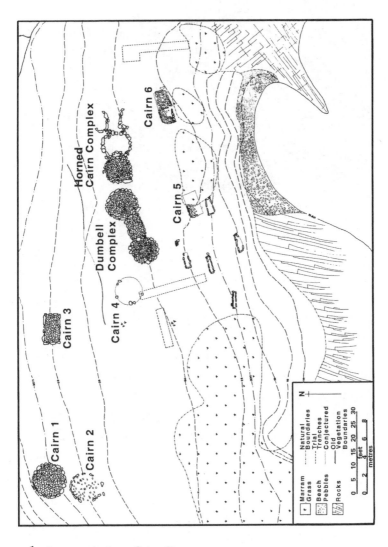

1 A general plan of the dig

2 A view of the figure-of-eight or 'dumbell' complex

structure was massively built, covered in rounded and angular stones.

Lying immediately to the east of this monstrosity was another rounded grave with a strange horseshoe-shaped entrance, very different from what had already been uncovered. It was 3.2 metres in diameter and 0.4 in height. There was a massive stone here, which would have been a grave marker, maybe rolled into position as a door. Another female body was interred here, obviously an important character in life judging from the grandeur of the grave.

Two further females were found in this horned cairn. The only metal find on the whole site was found in this cairn — an iron pin, which was found interred with the middle skeleton, rusted and with no obvious use. At a guess it could have held together a cloak or a cape, which has rotted away over the years leaving the rusty pin.

In all 22 bodies over an area of 30 square metres were exhumed, with many bone fragments, suggesting at least six more corpses had been buried here.

Two of the leaders gave their analysis of the dig, Iain H M Smart and Margaret Campbell Wilson. They wrote that twelve skeletons were thought to be definitely female and two more probably female. Four more were considered

3 The skeletal remains of a female aged 18 to 25, 161.5cm in height.

to be male and four more probably male. Six of the skeletons in the "Horned Cairn" complex were female, and one probably female. In the figure-of-eight-shaped cist complex, the middle cist contained a female and the lateral cists males. The twin cairns contained a male and a female. The three cists under rectangular cairns contained females and the scattered cists contained three males and one probable female.

The average height of the twelve definite females could be estimated as 5 foot one inch (155 cm) ranging from 4 foot ten (147 cm) to 5 foot 5 inches (165 cm).

Of the four definite males identified, average height was 5 foot 8 inches (173 cm), ranging from 5 foot 5 inches (165 cm) to 5 foot 10 (178 cm). The youngest skeleton was 18 years old and the oldest seemed to be around 45 years. The average age of all found was 25–30 years old.

4 The skeleton of a male, possibly aged from 40 to 50, and 178.5cm tall

5 The remains of a female 30 to 40 years old and 156cm in height

On inspection the condition of the teeth in all the examples found were staggeringly good. Several dental abscesses were found but generally they were in good condition. No evidence of congenitally missing teeth, apart from the possibility of third molars.

When inspected for traces of disease, the skeletons showed osteoarthritic changes in the lower vertebrae which were present in nine skeletons, in three cases to a severe degree. One skeleton had a fracture of the third lumbar vertebrae associated with the osteoarthritis; another showed signs of it in hip and sacroiliac joints. One body showed clear evidence of a healed fracture of the collarbone.

Carbon dating in 1970 and 1999 of fourteen of the bodies gave surprising results:

Human bone	figure-of-8 cairn	1300 BC–AD 400
Human bone	south horn of cairn cist	AD 600–1160
Human bone	cist A	AD 400–950
Human bone	cist G	AD 250–800
Human bone left femur	cist P	AD 340–560
Human bone	horned cairn	AD 400–540
Human bone	horned cairn	AD 420–600
Human bone	figure-of-8 cairn	AD 420–600
Human bone	horned cairn	AD 420–600
Human bone	horned cairn	AD 430–620
Human bone	rectangle cairn	AD 430–620
Human bone	round cairn	AD 540–660
Human bone	round cairn	AD 540–660

It was apparent after testing that the "Horned Cairn" complex held people from the same family group; the others scattered around the circumference had been buried within three or four generations of each other. What this shows is a community living in the Largo area from before the time of Christ, that buried its dead. The carbon dating confirmed that there has been human occupation here for over 3,000 years!

The Lundin Links cairn cemetery reflects a tradition that may have flourished throughout Scotland: a similar cemetery was found 23 kilometres away near St Andrews at a place called Kirkhill, another in Angus at Redcastle shows round domed cists similar to those found in Lundin Links.

I have done a lot of study of 16th-century activity along the Fife coasts, and from an early period these fishing communities were threading fishing lines using their teeth to soften the lines before tying hooks. This was a nightmare later on as teeth wore and cracked under the constant assault of the fishing lines. Teeth from corpses were much sought after, as they could be fastened into wooden blocks to make a very basic form of false teeth! Sheep's teeth were used but were found not to be very good. Armed guards were employed to stand in graveyards and corpses were enclosed in metal cages pegged into the ground. Once a body decomposed it was lowered into the grave and buried. Apparently tooth raiders left a body alone once it was rotten. An example of such a cage was reported to be still lying in Leven cemetery in 1960 (two kilometres from Lundin Links), but I'm very sure the tooth robberies had ended much earlier than this date.

The Lundin Links skeletons suggest that this method of baiting hooks was not in use back in the first millennium. From the examples of the skulls, they were probably farmers and breeders more than fishers, judging by the excellent state of their teeth. The osteoarthritis found in the lower back area of the spine shows our ancestors were hard working, constantly lifting heavy loads, as would be expected when labouring with farming and stock.

A basic medical knowledge is obvious from the collarbone fracture that was found. This area had been reset, nursed and healed.

These were the Pictish tribes the Roman geographer Ptolemy talked about, often mentioned by the Romans in their records as "painted people" from the elaborate tattoos they covered themselves in. In time another northen tribe would envelope the Pictish nation and eventually they would be known collectively as "Scots" (from AD 843). Unified behind the first King of Scots, Kenneth MacAlpin, the 34th recorded King of Dalriada (in Argyll), the Picts and Scots finally united as one.

Claudius Ptolemy was a Roman citizen from Egypt, (circa 100–170 AD). Ptolemy, who wrote in Greek, was employed by the Romans to map out accurately the areas and land under Roman rule. They were to be the most detailed maps available showing the tribes and rivers in different areas. He found and documented Caledonia (Scotland) to have thirteen distinctive tribes living around the country, of which most were resisting Roman rule at the time of his analysis. The two tribes in Fife he maps as the Veniconi in the East of Fife and the Horsetti tribe to the West. The graves from the carbon dating in Lundin

Links give rough dates leading us to presume fairly reliably that the cemetery was used extensively by members of the Veniconi tribe.

The Pictish nation was thought to stem from Ireland, and one story has it that when they made their invasion into Scotland they had hardly any women with them. A request was made to the Irish kings, who responded in kind, but with the wish that the Pictish line of kings would stem from the female line and that they would worship the females.

The Picts left no written records and what little has been explained of them has come from Roman records. They lived extensively in Fife having a capital in what now is now Markinch in central Fife. Many place names in Scotland have the prefix of "Pitt" in the name, eg Pittenweem, Pitlessie or Pitlochry. "Pitt" was a word in the Pictish language believed to mean a walled enclosure, and they prefixed their town-names with the word.

Many elaborate carved stones and items of jewellery have been excavated from Pictish settlements over the years by archaeologists. In Largo, during the construction of the railway line in 1848, two gold torques were found buried in the earth, directly behind a well on the railway line out by an area called Johnston's Mill. The torques were twisted braids of gold, designed to go round the neck and to hold a cape in place like a clasp. These torque finds show that there were people of standing in the habitation at Largo.

(The Pictish tribes would hide their valuables if they went to war or were invaded by enemies. Were these buried torques never recovered by the owners because they had been slain in battle with the Romans?)

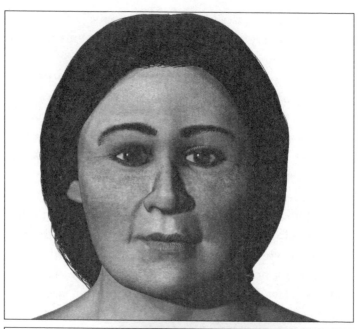

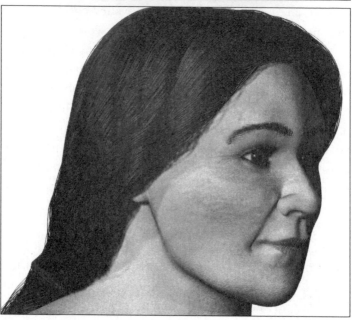

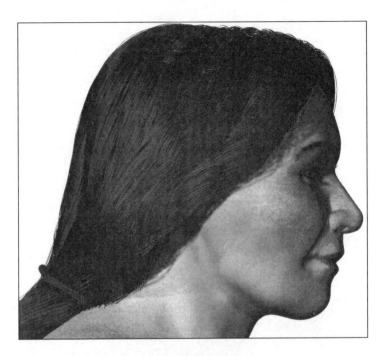

6 Dundee University put muscle and skin to the Lundin Links skeleton and came up with this face reconstruction of our Veniconi Pict woman

The example in Lundin Links of the cist graveyard suggests that the natives here did indeed worship the female, as the layout of the graves and sex of the grandest cists show us they had maximum importance. Was the tradition requested by the Irish kings — to worship the female — carried out without question? Lundin Links would appear to be a shrine to a female of great importance, maybe even a queen of a tribe. The team from Dundee took one of the skulls from the Lundin Links site and attempted a facial construction of the skull with muscle and skin added. Our Pictish woman, minus

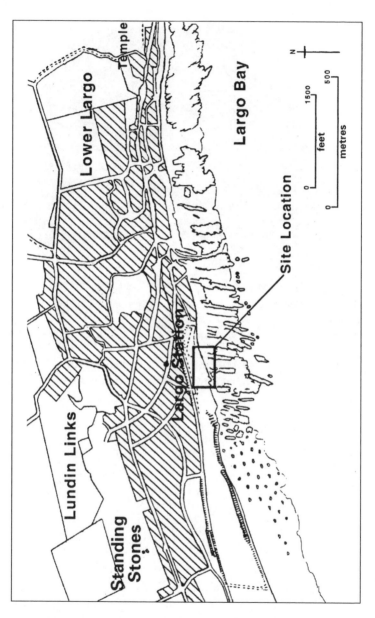

7 Map showing location of dig site in Largo

what tattoos she may have had, looks very nourished and pretty.

Close by, less than a kilometre north of the Pictish graveyard on the beach, there sits, on the drive of the first tee on today's Lundin Links ladies' golf course, a remnant of their religion.

There stand three huge stone monoliths (*see* cover). In moonlight they cast a sinister shadow over the flat land, standing nineteen feet high at the largest. They stand tripodlike, with as much of the stone below ground as shows above ground, to stabilize their weight. These examples of what appear to be significant memorials of pagan religions have appeared all over Scotland.

Sometimes the stones balance a fourth stone as a roof over the three others. A fourth stone of equal size was actually reported to be lying nearby on the ground in 1820, which could have served this purpose, but there is no trace of it today. It appears either to have sunk into the ground or to have been removed.

Some writers in the 1800s suggested that the Largo stones were gravestones to Danish chiefs killed in battle around King Macbeth's time, 1040–57; there is history to Macbeth's victory over the Danes along the Fife coast. When I was younger, along in Fife Ness to the furthest end of East Fife, along the beach there, my father pointed out a series of large flat stones, unusual in their position, but underneath them were human bones showing complete skeletons. I presume these were the resting places of the vanquished Danish army but no written evidence is on hand to enhance this theory.

According to one writer, there was a battle over both sides of the River Leven in which the Scottish King

Constantine II (c.879–952) fought the Viking chiefs Hubba and Horsa and defeated them. But it wouldn't make much sense to have a tribute to the victory at Lundin Links, which is too far away from where the battle was fought.

The stones are made of red sandstone, they were certainly not taken from the local beaches, as the sandstone is not typical. More probably they were quarried from inland sources and dragged by many oxen and men to this sacred position, and eventually forced upright into standing position.

It is recognised in Roman records that the people responsible for these monuments were called "Druids". The origin of the Latin term comes from the Celtic word "druidh" signifying a seer, wise man or magician, a meaning highly expressive of the character and profession of those primitive worshippers. The Romans under Emperor Claudius declared the Druidic practice illegal in AD 54; in AD 61 they met such religion in Britain face on with their army and massacred the opposition on their island — probably Anglesey.

The Druid priests supported the worship of moon and sun gods, and the Romans claimed that regular human sacrifices were carried out to honour their gods. Was the Picts' shrine in Lundin Links built by Druids or by even earlier people? Modern experts say Stonehenge was erected long before the Druids' time.

There are niches and recesses cut deep and far back in the standing rocks in Lundin Links, suggesting that it was designed to support a great weight. A fourth stone could have been the table-top piece that was originally held up by the other three stones.

8 Lundin standing stones

Moving to the early 14th century, we find Edward I of England continuing his war with the Scots, who were now under Robert the Bruce. Intending to strike fear into the Scots, Edward's army invaded, and desecrated many Scottish monuments on his incursion into Scotland, burning records and reportedly destroying a Roman temple that stood by the river Carron. It has been mentioned by previous writers in 17th-century Scotland (such as Buchanan) that King Edward destroyed the top stone at Lundin Links.

There are other tripod stones in Britain and on the Continent. What appeared to be a similar tripod stone with its lid on used to stand at Stenness in the Orkney Islands. The lid lay beside the tripod and had been restored in 1907 and then was toppled in 1972, and people are still arguing about those stones there.

Hector Boece was born in the middle of the 15th century. The first principal of Aberdeen University, Boece wrote many volumes on the early history of Scotland. Many scholars still reflect back on his work today for their own studies. He came down to Lundin Links from Aberdeen as a guest of the Lundin family not long after the disaster of Flodden field. Boece was escorted to the sacred site, where he stood by the stones. Just like us today, he would have wondered about their existence and what purpose and meaning the stones actually had to the masters who constructed them.

D Hay Fleming included a charming little lament to the stones in his book *Guide to the East Neuk of Fife*:

How came you here? Who bade you stand?
    Grim sentinels o'er sea and land
Did grateful nation you appear.
    In memory of a patriot dear?
Did some repulsed invader sue?
    For leave to lay his slain with you?
Or were your sides in days of yore
    Oft stained with sacrificial gore?
No picture, symbol nor a word
    You bear, to show what you record
Nor threat nor bribe can make you tell
    The secret that you keep so well.

A carved stone was found in Largo about a kilometre north from the Lundin Links standing stones. It is 2.5 metres long and was found in a field, broken in two by a farmer's plough. It bears a curved pattern with interlaced stonework. The strange figure of what looks like an elephant is present on one side, perhaps showing that they had knowledge of a beast not native to our country (there are no records of the Romans bringing elephants into Britain). With further study and a bit of guesswork from Pictish experts, this elephant image has now been found

9 The Largo Pictish Stone, showing both sides, the hunting scene shows just above the hunting dogs a beast with huge tusks

Bear?

Serpent and Head of Bull

Boar

Bull

10 Some Pictish symbols found in carvings in different parts of Scotland: the bear picture is similar to the one seen on the Largo stone

carved on at least 34 stones all over Scotland. It is identified as the image of a bear by some experts, but I'm not so sure. It has distinctive ears and a long curly tail, with a long trunk-like nose — there is nothing in this to identify it as a bear.

Because its image has been found all over Scotland it seems to have been a well-known animal. Other animals carved by the Picts are carved fairly exactly (*see* examples) so I would argue against the experts' opinion: the Largo stone carving looks nothing like a bear!

(Mammoth fossils dating back 10,000 years have been found extensively in parts of England. Is this an image carried into myth by the Pictish people?)

The carved stone now sits upright in a metal cage and may be viewed in Upper Largo church cemetery. It seems a shame that it is still open to the elements and shows more signs of wear. It would be more suited to an enclosed environment, so that it can be protected and held in awe for generations to come.

The Picts held the sun and moon in high esteem as gods to worship, and made their sacrifices, human and animal, to them. This was an age before Christianity. The Romans did not officially recognise Christianity till Emperor Constantine endorsed it in the lands of Roman occupation as the official religion in the 4th century. Scotland would remain wrapped in pagan gods till 563, when St Columba landed from Ireland and constructed a parish in Iona on the west coast of Scotland for Christian worship. He and St Fillan after him in the 8th century would set about converting the Picts to Christianity.

St Fillan has a cave named after him in Pittenweem, the town is probably named after a Pictish settlement, with "Pitt" as its prefix. In all probability it was St Fillan himself who converted the Picts along this Fife coast, and the Veniconi tribe.

Today famed for being the patron saint of mental illness, St Fillan was born with a horrific deformity of the mouth. Something that looked like a stone took the place of his tongue. It was thought that he would die not long after his birth in Munster, Ireland. His own father wanted to kill this monstrosity of a child, but the boy was deposited with monks instead, and they brought him up and taught him the Christian faith.

In my previous book *The Weem Witch*, I recount how Beatrix Laing, one of the Pittenweem witches, was locked in this dark forbidding cave for a period of five months, awaiting a date for her and seven others to be burnt as witches. I occasionally take tour parties into St Fillan's Cave and even during a summer's day it is pitch dark in there! To be locked up there for five months would test the sanity of any man. Beatrix was eventually released but was chased from the town of Pittenweem to die in the gutters of St Andrews of starvation and illness, as no one would take any care of an accused witch.

The St Fillan legend here states that he had a glowing "holy arm". If you imagine him writing, down in the cave, you can envisage him using a candle as illumination. It might seem from a distance that his arm itself was indeed glowing! He stayed in this cave and translated religious texts from Latin to English. After his death his "holy" right arm bone was kept in a silver casket, with the Abbott of Inchaffy Abbey as guardian.

In 1314 King Robert the Bruce asked for the relic to be brought on to the field of Bannockburn. Together with other holy relics, it had pride of place and witnessed the victory over the English. Now lost, it disappeared during the great upheaval of the Protestant reformation. St Fillan's crozier-head or "quigrich" was saved and can be viewed in the Museum of Scotland.

His cave in Pittenweem can be viewed by obtaining the keys from the coffee shop on the main street and is well worth a visit. Basically it is a cave within a cave about three metres high and goes back thirty metres. As I have already pointed out, it is pitch dark in there, be it day or night, and a family of bats shares it with the ghosts of the past. I find the cave relaxing, and it interests me that St Fillan is the patron saint of mental illness. That's probably why I'm so relaxed in there!

Chapter 2

The Largo Picts Fight Roman Occupation

In the year AD 84, the Roman general Agricola in his seventh campaign gathered his 9th legion army, crossed the River Leven into Fife and advanced to a place which is known as Scotlandwell nowadays.

Then the army turned north-east, through to the higher grounds of the other side of the Vale of Eden. By the time the Roman army had formed up on the lands of Edenshead they were shocked to find they had a full view of the whole Caledonian army standing facing them. Corbred II, more commonly known as Calgacus, was the Celtic chief. Angered by Roman invasion and hostility in his land he gathered the tribes together in a joint fight for their existence against this Roman threat. All the tribes that Ptolemy had mapped out now showed support in arms against the Roman host, including no doubt the Largo-based Veniconi — North-East Fife Picts.

This at any rate was the scenario described by Rev Andrew Small in a fascinating book written early in the 19th century. Many Roman remains had been found in

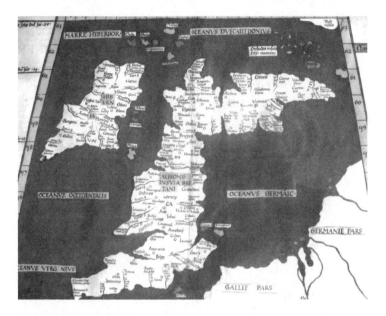

11 The Roman map of Britain by Ptolemy, where you can see the Veniconi lands in Fife mapped out, in which he has got the shape of Fife almost correct

Fife, but they were not highly valued, and Small knew of manmade mounds that had disappeared because they had been used for building materials, and of other discoveries that had not been preserved.

According to Small, he had written his description of the great Roman battle in his neighbourhood before reading Tacitus's account of it. When he came to read Tacitus's work, he was more than ever convinced that he had identified the site of the battle between Calgacus and Agricola, and that the battle of Meralsford, supposed to have been with the Saxons or the Danes, was in fact this battle between the Romans and the Caledonians. The dead, according to him, were burnt in four different places, and great cairns were erected over them. Mounds were built to mark the battle site. Roman battle axes were discovered in the area, also bronze vessels and many urns, as well as coins of the Emperor Domitian.

It was Small's view that Tacitus's Calgacus was the Corbred II mentioned by the historian Buchanan. Small conceived of the Roman legions marching round the east side of the Lomond Hills, by Scotlandwell and Balgedie and meeting the Caledonians somewhere along the Eden with immense slaughter. He wrote, "That it was so, the ground all along where the battle had raged gives abundant proof, notwithstanding the extraordinary lapse of 1,700 years, by vast quantities of bones, half burnt, ashes of bones, pieces of iron, beads, broken urns, &c. which are yet frequently turned up by the plough, even after the general burning of the dead, which the Romans always practised, and which was evidently done in all the other places where the battle raged."

Small believed that the course of the battle was aferwards marked by large cairns. "The retreat of the Roman army across it [the Eden], about two and a half miles to the west, was clearly pointed out, till of late, by the large cairn at the place where the battle commenced, running in a straight line over to another cairn on the south side of the river, which, I believe, is still remaining on the east side of the farm of Easter Gospetrie, a little to the eastward of a dark fir planting."

There was another large cairn on the west side of the western farm of Nether Urquharts. Small blamed the destruction of these cairns on land enclosures: "All these ancient remains of Roman antiquity have fallen a sacrifice to the great rage that took place for inclosing lands about thirty years ago, or even within a less period as to some of them." Small was quite sure that the cairns marked the progress of the Romans in battle: "Had all these cairns still stood, on both sides of the river, they would have still pointed out to the attentive observer all the movements of the Roman army almost as exactly as though he had been an eye-witness."

He noted the amazing survival of traditions about the battle: "The slaughter here seems to have been so dreadful, that, even after the extraordinary lapse of seventeen centuries, the common tradition of the country bears — and seems to be as fresh in the mouths both of old and young as though the battle had been fought only a hundred years ago — that, after this battle, the river Eden ran red with blood for two days!"

According to Small, to the south of where, in his time, a spinning mill stood, an "immense number of the ashes of burnt bones" were found "lying in large pits in the form of stone coffins, and covered with thin broad flags ... There was also a very large cairn laid upon these; and the proprietor lately told me that when removing the stones, besides the ashes already mentioned, there was also a pit of pure fine sand by itself, about as fine as is usually put into sand-glasses, which he thinks had been used for regulating the fire in burning of the dead."

When Small himself visited the spot he calculated was the site of the battle, he found human bones dug up by moles, which he believed to be those of the "brave Caledonians". He wrote: "happening to pick up one about two inches square, a piece of the sternum or breast-bone, after being exposed to the action of the weather for about 1737 years, I took it carefully home with me." He was worried that he might have disturbed the "genii" of the battle site, as he was visited in his dreams more than once by Napoleon (then still alive)!

There was another large cairn which stood in the grounds of Wellfield. When it was removed, "a vast number of urns full of ashes were found, which the workmen called cans, and many of them finely carved; some more coarsely than others. ... The greater part were broken and demolished by the men ... If we could be certain that the Romans did always, or even in general, inhume the ashes of their dead in urns, then it plainly appears that the slaughter among their troops had been so great as even to make them run short of, or to produce an absolute scarcity of urns among them; because a great number of stone coffins full of ashes of burnt bones were found in the immediate neighbourhood of the cairn, when trenching and improving the ground. ... There was also a stone coffin found a little south from the cairn, when digging a ditch for a stripe of planting, on the road side, containing a very large skeleton at full length, with uncommonly large teeth; but, whenever it was exposed to the atmospheric air, or touched, it crumbled down into dust. This, I think, had evidently been a person of distinction among the Romans, as it, as well as the urns and other stone coffins, were all in the immediate vicinity of the great cairn. ... What a noble monument of Roman antiquity! but now, alas! gone with all the rest of those ancient monuments. The proprietor told me that there were more stones in this cairn than built a rood of dyke [1,040 square metres]! He also mentioned, that there was a capacious pit dug to the depth of about four yards [3.65m], containing an immense quantity of ashes of burnt bones and charred wood, intermixed with layers of pure white sand; then, a large quantity of stones thrown on irregularly; then a regular pavement of stones above these, on which were placed small leaden coffins about two feet long, all full of burnt bones. Each of these leaden coffins, amounting in all to seven, had a long stone erected on end above them, but so supported as not to press too hard upon the coffins; and, though the lead was fully the thickness of two inches [5cm], yet it was very much wasted."

Small was sure that the ashes found in this area came from the Romans: "Though we have lost much by the demolition of these noble monuments of Roman antiquity, yet, by the opening of these, we have got a more confirming evidence, by the burning of the dead, that this was actually done by the Romans; as it was they alone, in our island, who burned their dead."

He recorded the removal of standing stones and the finding of more urns in the area: "One of peculiar elegance and superior workmanship was dug up, which indicates that it contained the ashes of some officer of distinction among the Romans."

Roman historian Gaius Cornelius Tacitus (AD 56–117) tells us that Julius Agricola had been sent to Britain as Governor, under Emperor Vespasian's reign in AD 78. He subdued in battle the Ordovices (from north-west Wales) and took Anglesey by force. His second year he campaigned north. He was a renowned master in the art of fortification; many buildings were constructed during his winter stops. The fortifications were designed for all year round habitation with firm defences in place. His further campaigns north brought him to the River Tweed where he fixed a permanent camp in his third year then, seeing the Rivers Clyde and Forth so close, he made plans for a wall of forts to be constructed between the two areas.

In his fourth campaign in AD 81 he subdued the natives between the Tweed and the Forth and Clyde (the Romans named them Bodotria and Glotta). The wall was started by Lollius Urbicus and finished by Antoninus Pius whose name was eventually given to the 50-kilometre earthen wall.

Parts of this construction still stand nearly 2,000 years since its build. I have seen stretches of the Antonine Wall at the back of Bonnybridge near Falkirk and it is indeed still impressive.

In his sixth year he ventures into Fife across the River Forth (Bodotria); camps were struck at Dumfermline and Burntisland. It was here his scouts came with news of a Celtic army under Calgacus uniting the Picts and other tribes. The Celts attacked at Lochore, were beaten back but not defeated as they shadowed the army and attacked again at Meralsford.

The Romans called this battle Mons Graupius or Grampius, and because of this some historians have placed this battle in the Grampian region south-west of Aberdeen, but it was not so. Andrew Small writing in 1823 studied the battlefield at the foot of the Lomonds as described above and matched the battle layout to the Roman description of the battle. His words follow:

"Upon the armies approaching each other, Galgacus, commander of the Islanders, represents to them: 'That every thing that was valuable to them, their lives, their liberties, their properties, and privileges, and the lives of their wives, and children, and other relations, and everything that was dear to them was at stake, and that, being at the extremity of the Isle, they have no refuge left if vanquished; and, therefore, nothing but victory can deliver them from perpetual bondage.' On the other side, Agricola exhorts his soldiers 'to do their duty, by the consideration of their past victories. Particularly, he sets before their eyes their sad condition, if, after being defeated, they are forced to seek for shelter among the Britons, who, for fifty years together, have felt the force of their victorious arms.'"

According to Tacitus, the Roman army was drawn up so that the 8,000 or so auxiliary infantry were to bear the first shock of the Caledonian charge. There were 3,000 Roman cavalry on the wings. The legionaries (who could have been as many as a further 18,000 men) were stationed in the rear.

The Caledonians were ranged on the side of the hill, so that his whole army could be viewed by the Romans, to strike terror into them at his force's size. War chariots and horses could be seen careering about in the centre of the Celts.

Agricola, apprehensive of being flanked by the bigger army, widened his front to match the multitudes. He then came down from his horse to take his position on foot beside the Roman standards.

The Caledonians were equipped with slashing swords and small shields (targets), that were of little use in such close contact because they had no stabbing point on the swords, which were blunt-ended, while the Romans' short stabbing swords were made for such close encounters.

Agricola detached two cohorts of Batavians and as many more Tungrians (both types of natives from what we now know as Holland) into the attack. Massed and squashed against each other, the stabbing action of the Romans began to thin the Caledonian lines. They were being pushed up the hill on the points of the auxiliaries' swords.

The Celts' horse chariots tried to engage unsuccessfully. More Celts came down from where they had been watching from nearby hilltops, but Agricola threw his mounted horse against them and made great slaughter here. The Celts fell back in disorder leaving the dead in heaps where the fighting had been hardest. There were some attacks on Roman pursuers as they entered the woods, but Agricola made sure the Romans advanced in good order and the Celts scattered. The battle was won. According to Tacitus, 10,000 Celts had been killed for the loss of 360 Romans.

Andrew Small was certain that this battle took place near the Lomond Hills, and disputed the small number of Roman casualties from the evidence of clay urns holding the ashes of their dead. Also if Agricola had achieved such a complete victory, why did he head south, never to return? Historians have hinted a suggestion of maybe 3,400 Roman dead is a more probable estimate.

The Romans never ventured further north into the Highlands. In legend, the famous 9th Legion was portrayed as marching into the Highlands and vanishing! Not a trace of 6,000 troops! Two films from Hollywood came out not long ago, *The Eagle* and *Centurion*, depicting the Celts attacking and wiping them out. There is no actual evidence that this ever happened.

12 An imaginative representation of Roman legionaries fighting the ancient inhabitants of Scotland

But the Roman expansion stopped, so fiercely fought by the Celts' army they ventured no further north.

Tacitus records that Agricola marched back to the Horsetti lands in Western Fife. He had never met such a formidable opponent as Calgacus and his hardy

Caledonians containing Scots from the northern territories and Picts from the south. His thoughts must have been that to venture further north might be the complete ruin of his army.

The Romans set up camp in Fife for a while, and they had a base at close quarters to the Veniconi Picts of Lundin Links. Andrew Small wrote about a 1795 discovery here. He wrote that a farm worker in Hatton on the estate of Lundin Castle in Lundin Links, while ploughing on the hill Hatton Law, about 400 metres north east of Lundin House, struck a large stone. A man was employed to take it out, and after loosening it, he was amazed to see it fall down into an underground house. After making a big enough entrance, he ventured into it. The house had once been inhabited, as there were several household utensils in it. It was a vaulted arched room built of yellowish unburnt limestone, without any lime or cement used in the brick.

Many people came to see the underground house at that time, and they saw an old bronze kettle of Roman type; there was also the tusk of a wild boar, 15 centimetres in length, and its jaw. Some knives and forks were found but much rusted and a huge carving knife. It was noted that the front door entered from the south east on the side of the hill, and the stonework to the doorframe was very low and built of the same yellow stone. The stone door frames showed much wear where knives and swords had been sharpened upon the doorway, confirming that the house had been lived in.

(Apparently those same stone door frames were subsequently used as stepping-stones over a dry-stone dyke in a footpath leading from Lundin Mill up to the old Castle of Balcruivie.)

This was part of the remains of the Roman camp of Lindum, in Andrew Small's view, and he thought that it could have been named after Lindum in the south (i.e. Lincoln), possibly because of a similar situation on the south-facing slope of a hill. Over the years the name slightly changed to Lundin, now Lundin Links.

I myself have been up to have a look at where the camp stood on Hatton Law and you can definitely make out the outline of it.

The underground house alas was destroyed on the orders of Lundin Castle; a local man called Neil Adamson was employed in the destruction of this relic. By coincidence, a man known to the author Andrew Small lived at that time next door to the subterranean house and was alive in 1818 to relay the story to him, and otherwise the Roman camp location would have been lost to history.

Chapter 3

The Pirate Sir Andrew Wood

In Scotland's long list of patriots, one man rarely gets much more than a footnote in passing. Throughout the history books, great heroic stories depict the exploits of William Wallace, Robert the Bruce, The Earl of Montrose, Rob Roy McGregor and Bonnie Prince Charlie in the history of the Scottish nation. Sir Andrew Wood's achievements actually eclipse most of the above. He held the favour of two Scottish kings, he won incredible honours in battle, he held the Scottish flag unfurled to show the world that Scotland did have a navy, a forceful navy, as those foolish enough to test it found out to their bloody cost!

Wood was absolutely devoted to his king, and garnered more plaudits than any before him, risking his life against incredible odds at sea and land. As a Largo man, he is sadly overshadowed and forgotten, with another famous son Alexander Selkirk (Robinson Crusoe) much better known. Although Alexander Selkirk does have a chapter later on in this book, how is it that a bigamist, brawling, argumentative drunk can take pride of place over

Sir Andrew Wood and his achievements? I can only shake my head in disbelief that no proper memorial exists to the man. In Upper Largo church, under the floorboards where the piano now stands, lies the body of Sir Andrew Wood. It's been resting there nearly five hundred years now. It was exposed a few years back when the worn flooring under the piano was replaced, and people saw the skeleton of the great man briefly, before the floor was repaired once again. Sir Andrew Wood is one of the very few of Scotland's military heroes who actually died in his bed!

The grandfather of my old school friend Bruce Marshall, who lived in Largo, made a replica of Sir Andrew Wood's flagship, "the yellow caravel", and it sits near his grave in the church. I take great honour in relaying this great man's history.

We have no birth date for this illustrious man, but most records suggest it was in the mid 1400s. Born in the Kirkton of Upper Largo, Wood's early days are a mystery to us, but his mark in history is first made as a merchant ship trader, with his ships based at Edinburgh's harbour at Leith. He commanded two ships of about 300 tonnes, the *Yellow Caravel* and the *Flower*. Both traded with the Dutch and Hanse (German) towns, delivering wool and hides, and returning with cartwheels, wheelbarrows, small silk and linen items, and buttons and needles, which were in huge demand in the Scottish market.

The caravel was a three-masted sailing vessel with square rigging, It had a roundish hull with a high bow and stern. The name "caravel" came from its method of construction, which was a change from the bulkier merchant ships of old. The Portuguese invented the caravel method of build in the 15th century for exploration. In 1492, Christopher Columbus's flagship the *Santa Maria* was a typical caravel-type ship.

In 1481 Edward IV of England had sent a fleet up from Harwich to attack Scotland, under the command of Sir John Howard. Andrew Wood bravely attacked and saw off the English ships, which appeared in the Firth of Forth. Both sides claimed victory. Not long afterwards, Wood also successfully defended Dumbarton when the castle there was besieged by the fleet of Edward IV.

For his actions James III of Scotland granted Wood lands in Largo and "for his eminent services on land and sea, in peace and war a charter under the great seal to him and his heirs in fee". He was knighted and James IV confirmed the charter again to him after he succeeded to the throne.

Sir Andrew Wood is famed in the history of his country, as much for his faithful adherence to his sovereign when abandoned by his nobles, as for his courage and naval skill.

Prior to 1487 he appears to have entirely relinquished trading as a merchant, and to have entered into the service of the crown. Early in 1488, when rebellious nobles had collected an army and marched towards the capital with the young James, James III's son, as representative against his father. King James took refuge in the *Yellow Caravel* anchored in the bay of Leith. His rebellious son and nobles stood in arms against him and in strength of more than 20,000 men at arms. The King in quieter moments, shared his feeling with his most loyal subject. With his own son at the head of an army facing him, there must have been dark thoughts in that room. What was said was taken to the grave by both men.

The king left the ship, his soldiers loyal to him formed ranks, and order for battle was prepared. Captain Wood was under orders to be waiting off the coastline, ready to carry his king to safety should the forthcoming battle turn sour for him.

On 11 June 1488, the King's forces of 30,000 men at arms faced his son's revolutionaries on the field of Sauchieburn.

Andrew Wood had married Elizabeth Lundie, the daughter of John Lyndsay, so was related by marriage to the master of Pittcruvie castle, his good friend Robert Lyndsay.

Lyndsay was, like Wood, a supporter of the king, but his two younger sons had joined the rebellion. The day before the battle Robert Lyndsay had presented the King with a sturdy grey horse, with words to the effect that it would speed the king to safety in his hour of need. The two armies fought, father on one side and his son against him with his army. The King, having no heart for the battle against his own son, was thrown from the horse during the fight. The fight was going against him and his army was losing. Injured, he rode out of the battlefield and slumped against a mill near Bannockburn. His intent was to travel towards where Wood's ship and safety lay waiting for him. When a man in priest's clothing approached, the King cried out for help, but the priest, recognising his monarch, duly produced a sword and stabbed him, ending his life on the spot.

Andrew Wood had the *Yellow Caravel* and the *Flower* just off the coast; his two brothers John and Robert kept watch on shore with some men at arms in case the King's approach was followed, and assistance would be given in sharing the dangers of the day. But of course the King was already slain and lying in a ditch with his throat torn from him, blighting his decorative attire and the valiant art of his royal dress.

The victors of the battle of Sauchieburn advanced to Linlithgow, and a report reached the rebel camp that Andrew Wood's ships were off the coast taking survivors of the battle on board. There was every reason to suggest to them the King himself had boarded for his safety, for his true fate was then unknown. The rebels quickly moved to Leith, when in view of the ships a messenger was put on board in the name of James the Duke of Rothesay, the son of James III, to inquire after His Majesty's person. Andrew Wood answered "he was not aboard the ships, and to have free leave to search". A second message was sent requesting an interview in person, on condition the rebels left the Lords Seaton and Fleming on board the ships as hostages for his safe return.

On Andrew Wood's appearance in his splendid full armour in front of the rebels' council, the young Prince James, all of sixteen years old and emotionally torn at the sight of the figure before him fell in tears asking, "Sir, are you my father?"

Wood lifted his visor so the young prince would be mistaken no more, and replied, "I am not your father but his faithful servant, and the enemy of all who have occasioned his downfall"

"Know you where the king is?" asked the committee and, "Who have you taken on board after the battle?"

Wood answered, "he knew nothing of the King's whereabouts but he and his brothers were ready to risk our lives in his defence, boats had been launched and beached waiting for the King as planned, but there had been no sign of his coming". Fiercely he boasted to the committee, "if the king is alive, he was resolved to obey none but him. And if he had fallen slain, he was ready to avenge him." Again he was asked if the king was hiding on board, and replied, "I wish to God he was, for then he would be in safety. Then I would defend him from these vile traitors, who I fear may have slain him and whom, I hope to see, one day, rewarded as they deserve" (this is recorded by Robert Lyndsay of Pitscottie).

After a while Wood was allowed to withdraw to his ship unmolested, to the relief of his brothers who were worried at the long absence and were preparing to launch a war party for his rescue.

Once he was on board, the hostages Lord Seaton and Fleming were released. Upon hearing of the results of the meeting and the way Wood had spoken to them, Seaton flew into a fury and resolved to punish Andrew Wood for his insolence. The masters of all of Leith's fishing and trading fleet were summoned and council was taken to send them all against Wood to punish and subdue him, offering lucrative rewards for his capture. There was no agreement to any such action: they all declined. Barton, a sea captain, mentioned to the council "the two ships were all so well equipped with all things for fighting, and so well furnished with able and valiant seamen, and with all that, a captain so skilled in naval affairs and so practised in war that ten of the best ships in Scotland could not cope with his two".

The action was called off, and reluctantly abandoned. King James's death was soon confirmed, but for a while Wood in his grief for his lost monarch refused to give adherence to the newly proclaimed James IV. For the rest

13 The author with the last remaining tower of Sir Andrew Wood's castle in Largo; there is a 4-metre drop over the wall (where the child is sitting). You can see how high the walls originally were from the broken stone against the tower, this was once a mighty stronghold. From the other side you can appreciate the scale the building once was.

of his life James IV would remember the actions that took his father's life, wearing a chain tight to his skin round his waist, in penance.

It was during James IV's reign, in 1490, that England's king Henry VII sent a raiding party to test the mettle of the new Scots king. Five English frigates made their way up the west of Scotland, attacking shipping in the Clyde, and then sailing north round Scotland to create mayhem on the country's eastern side.

A council was called, with orders to Sir Andrew Wood to make haste and chase those who threaten our borders. "What a shame dishonour and loss it was that a few English ships should ride under our eyes with impunity, committing every outrage and excess". Wood prepared his ships for war and hoisted sail to find the invaders. They were found off Dunbar and battle commenced. Before long all five English decks had been brutally mauled by cannon shot. The battle lasted a day, but was so one-sided that all five struck their colours and were berthed at Leith Harbour and presented to the King.

After the battle, Admiral Sir Andrew Wood was granted lands in Largo. He was given a charter under the great seal of Scotland to "build a castle in Largo, with gates of iron", as reward for great service done and in compensation for the losses sustained by him in service.

A four-towered castle was built, with additional housing, and English slaves were used in its construction. It was built on to an ancient edifice which had formerly been a dower house of Scottish queens.

Back in England news of the latest defeat, and that the name Wood again had soiled the flag of England, didn't go down well with King Henry. He was determined to assert his naval reputation and offered a bounty of £1,000 a year to any of his commanders who would capture Admiral Wood's ships and bring him back to England.

One man answered the King's call — Captain Stephen Bull. Other more worthy captains turned the offer down. Wood's name meant something. Many ships flying the English flag had fallen, and their crews were taken into slavery or in prison waiting for ransoms to be paid. Many a wife would never see her husband again.

Stephen Bull gathered three warlike ships and prepared them for battle with hardened crews and weaponry. The King's orders were to "bring this Admiral Wood to the English court, dead or alive". With his three ships Bull sailed down the River Thames in July 1490, with a great send-off, and headed for the Firth of Forth. He hid his ships behind the shadow of the Isle of May and waited for sight of the Scottish ships. All was unknown to Sir Andrew Wood; the English court had worked in secrecy to send this force up to Scotland. Sir Andrew had gone on merchant business to Flanders, as he thought there was peace between the two crowns of Scotland and England.

Stephen Bull attacked and took prisoners from some fishing crews from the local harbours. Their fish was stolen to feed the English crews full of soldiers. Some of the Scots fishermen were held on each of the three ships to identify the Admiral's *Yellow Caravel* and the *Flower* if they came into view.

At St Abb's Head down the coast, two frigates flying the Scottish flag appeared on the distant horizon. The captive fishermen hesitated to describe and identify the ships as Wood's. But they were promised their immediate liberty by Stephen Bull if they did so. Once confirmed, battle stations on all the English ships were beat out on drums on board, and the sailors and armed boarding parties made ready for war. Stephen was as good as his word and released the fishermen back to their boats.

The three English warships now exposed themselves from behind the Isle of May, barring Sir Andrew's passage into the Forth. On board the *Yellow Caravel*, Admiral Wood saw the threat, called his men and captains together and cried to them, "These my lads, are the foes who expect to convey us in bonds to the English King, but, by your courage and the help of God, they shall fail. Set yourselves in order, every man to his station. Charge gunners; let the crossbows be ready; have the lime pots and fire balls to the tops; and the two-handed swords to the fore room. Be stout, be diligent for your own sakes, and for the honour of this realm". A great cry from the men broke out at this speech and wine was handed around the crew, as armour and axe were readied for the bloody mêlée that was promised.

The sun was high, and the English strength glinted with steel, a huge crowd had gathered on the shores of Fife to watch this brawl between the five mighty ships.

Admiral Wood got to windward of the English fleet. His guns raked across the English decks which were packed with soldiers: in an instant whole companies of men were wasted, blown overboard and bodies splintered by the loose shot from the Scottish cannon. Smoke billowed and confusion ran high. The odds in numbers were now easily matched, the decks splashed with the smell of gore, and dead and dying on board the English ships. The ships stood apart, both sets of cannon in action, but the English guns were firing high trying to rip the masts down upon the Admiral's *Yellow Caravel*, with more thought to capturing its captain than winning the day. The Scots had to make no such calculation and fought for their own lives, motivated by fury at this rude attack when the two countries were meant to be at peace.

Night fell and ropes were cut to allow these two adversaries to rest and treat their wounded. As dawn came they crashed together again and the brutal brawl continued. The current brought the ships around the tip of Fife past St Andrews and into the Firth of Tay.

On the shore an army was now following the ships as they fought, marching around the coastline waiting for the ships to ground and take prisoner the English occupants.

It finally happened in the Tay: the three English vessels beached on the rocks and surrendered to Sir Admiral Wood. The bloody day was won.

Stephen Bull and his officers were taken to Edinburgh Castle and presented to King James IV. They were treated very well and handsomely honoured for their bravery; they were given gifts and sent back to England to Henry VII with the message: "Scotland, like England, could boast of brave and warlike sons both by land and sea, that England should no more disturb the Scottish seas, else a different fate would hereafter await the intruders".

Henry would eventually receive this message and refer to Admiral Wood as "nothing but a Scottish pirate".

Some years later, Sir Andrew saw more armed conflict, this time with a rebel chief from the Western Isles. In May 1503 he laid siege to the Castle of Cairnburg on one of the Treshnish Isles. With his lieutenant Robert Barton he reduced the castle and took all inside prisoner to the King.

King James IV was ambitious enough to see that investing in the Scottish Navy was essential for stability of the crown. A great warship was built at Leith at Newhaven dock — it was to be greater than anything the French or English fleets had ever owned. It was named the *Great Michael* after the Archangel Michael. It was 1,000 tonnes in weight and masses of timber in Fife was collected for her build until the forests were barren of oak trees, and then more was collected from oak forests in Norway.

She was to be 73 metres in length, and 11 metres wide, her sides were three metres thick and able to deflect any artillery of the day that was brought against her. The *Great Michael* carried 36 cannon and three handheld cannons on the decks. Her crew of 300 sailors had also 120 gunners aboard and she was designed to carry a thousand armed men on decks as well. She had four huge masts, held 21 flag pennants and 92 arrow shields all along the rim of the ship. All in all, a mighty and impressive ship; the English equivalent at the time was the flagship the *Mary Rose* which was half the size. The ship was finished in 1511 and under charge of Sir Andrew Wood and Robert Barton.

The captaincy of the ship would only be a year in Sir Andrew Wood's hands before being handed to Henry Lord Sinclair.

It is believed that the *Great Michael* was armed with a most formidable weapon, the 560mm cannon named "Mons Meg", which could fire 180-kilo cannon balls at a range of three kilometres. It was the biggest calibre weapon ever in its day, and even today when you look at the battleships of the Second World War the largest calibre naval guns were the 460mm guns on the Japanese battleship *Yamato*. The *Michael*, launched in 1512, probably had a bigger cannon than that, and if true, it's a proud boast that the biggest calibre gun ever at sea was Scottish.

In 1514 James IV answered a plea for help from the Queen of France: under attack from England she called for help from Scotland. At the head of a huge army James invaded England, and at first had some military success. Then he met the English at Flodden Field. On the high ground and having the advantage, he foolishly decided to move his army down the hill to face the English. His advantage was lost, his cannon couldn't depress downwards from the hill to aim at the enemy, and his men lost their footing on the slippery slope.

Once the two forces were on level ground, the clansmen on his right wing charged. The Highlanders crashed into the wall of English with broadsword and dirk working to such good effect at close quarters that the English broke away and retreated. As the Highlanders picked rewards from the dead, the English stopped and shot arrows into them to great effect. The Highlanders charged again and killed a great many of the enemy and they broke and retreated.

But it was in the centre where there was a weakness in the Scottish army. James had equipped the majority of his men with 6-metre pikes. They had no defence against archers and were clumsy and they were useless at close quarters. The English soldiers were equipped with metre-long swords known as bills, with which they cut the heads from the mass of pikes. The English carved their way through the Scots pikemen, who were left with nothing to defend themselves with but wooden poles, and reached the King's position.

They fought to a standstill, but by then the battle was won. James IV lay dead, along with many of his nobles and 10,000 of his subjects. There was no shambles of a retreat, as the Scots and English backed off and both held their ground. There were 5,000 English dead, but with the loss of the nobles, it was without question a national disaster for Scotland.

With the destruction of the Scottish nobility at Flodden Field, the *Great Michael* was sailed to France before it could fall into English hands and was sold to Louis XII for 40,000 livres, being half her build price. The ship was renamed the *Grand Nef d'Ecosse* or the "Big Ship of Scotland".

Scotland's new monarch James V was just two weeks old. Andrew Wood sailed again to France to collect the new regent, John the Duke of Albany, who was the nephew of James III.

In 1526 the Earl of Lennox attempted to rescue the young King from the dominance of the Douglases — this resulted in the battle of Linlithgow Bridge. Sir Andrew Wood was asked by the King to protect Lennox, but the request was sent too late and by the time the Admiral got on the field of battle Lennox had already been killed on the point of Douglas's sword.

Sir Andrew at a great old age finally retired to his castle in Largo and had a deep canal dug so that his men could row him to church from his keep. The canal would have been about 600 metres long. Today in heavy rain you can still see the outline of where it stood when water fills the void in the field across from the cemetery in Largo. He lived to a good old age, dying in his eighties, in 1540. His body was interred under the floor of Upper Largo Church. There is a plaque on the floor inside the church to commemorate him — sadly, it lies between two pews. There is also the model of his ship "the yellow caravel" made by the grandfather of a good friend of mine (Bruce Marshall), but the church is usually locked to the public, and so it's not so easy to get access, which is a shame.

Today, near where the First World War memorial stands on the coastal road in Lundin Links, two hundred metres up the road there is a farm where Sir Andrew Wood's castle used to stand. All that remains to be seen now of his four-tower castle is one of the conical towers, that still stands fairly dominant, having been built 500 years ago: a majestic feature in what would have been a mighty keep.

Sir Andrew Wood was a brave warrior, a skilful naval commander, an able accountant with an intimate knowledge of foreign commercial transactions. Befriended by three Scottish kings, he was a patriot and a hero, and is today one of Scotland's most forgotten sons. A marble slab was placed in the wall of his old castle in 1832 by General James Durham of Largo. It read:

These are the remains of the royal residence,
Granted with the lands of Largo by James the Third,
To his Admiral Sir Andrew Wood,
Who repaired and strengthened the fortalice by the hands of Englishmen captured by him.
This donation from his grateful sovereign,
Was the well merited reward of his brave and generous conduct,
In successfully defending at his own private expense,
The seas and shores of Scotland,
From the otherwise unconquered Navy of England.

The marble stone today has vanished but the legend has been carved into the wall of sandstone outside the last remaining tower. Although weathered, the writing can just be made out today.

The Wood family and their generations to come continued to serve Scotland's monarchs. Sir Andrew's son, John Wood, served James V's son James Stewart. His great grandson, also called John Wood, born in 1587, was a part of the household of James VI and Charles I. Money was bequeathed to build a hospice in Largo from John's will: it became Woods Hospital. The original building was damaged in a storm, and a newer sturdier building stands in its place today.

Robert Wood — Under Secretary of Scotland 1705–26 (6th generation)

John Wood — Governor of the Isle of Man 1761–77 (7th generation)

Captain John Wood — 1812–1871 Born Kilrenny, Fife. Discovered the source of the River Oxus in Asia.

Doctor Alexander Wood — a nine times grandson of the great Admiral Wood. Born 1817, died 1884, lived in Colinsburgh near Largo. He was appointed to the Royal College of Physicians of Edinburgh and is remembered as the inventor of the hypodermic syringe in 1853.

Sir Alan Muir Wood — tunnelling engineer — revolutionised the way roads and rail are now used. Built and designed the Clyde Tunnel, Tyne Tunnel, Second Mersey tunnel and the Great Fish River tunnel in South America — died in 2009 aged 87

Sir Ian Wood — industrialist — one of the first to recognise the importance of North Sea oil in Aberdeen discoveries, now a multibillion-pound empire employing 22,000 people.

Chapter 4

Witches

In 1484 two Dominican priests in Germany, one master, Jacob Sprenger, and his apprentice, Heinrich Krämer, changed a phrase in a book that would result in the pain and suffering of countless thousands from the moment their quill left the page. The actual death toll from these men's actions is beyond count, but when, three hundred years later, repeal laws ended the witch hunts, they left behind a lasting scar and embarrassment on the Catholic and Protestant faiths that even now won't heal.

The two priests were smarting in hatred for the abilities of people who actually practised the pagan and Wiccan faiths of old. They used recipes for medicines and maternity skills that were hundreds of years old and were still bearing fruit in Catholic communities. But prayer was the only medicine expected to heal the sick in the eyes of these religious monks, and with spiteful eyes they wanted the repugnance of the old faiths to be cleansed once and for all time. They wanted a holy purge where only one true God would reign over the faiths of old.

In the chapters of the bible, *Exodus* 22.18, the old Hebrew edition stated "thou shalt not suffer a poisoner to live" ... One slight change in translation and it became "thou shalt not suffer a witch to live". It was printed on the John Gutenberg printing press, in the new German edition of the Bible.

Following the printed edition of the Bible came the *Malleus Maleficarum*, a book that would bring so much calamity and terror to the modern world.

The *Malleus Maleficarum* was a book on torture, a book on finding, identifying and torturing witches to confess and destroying them in the name of God! A book with whole chapters on methods of torture, and ridiculous passages backing their methods such as "women were made from the rib of Adam, the rib is bent therefore so are women, whose faiths wander and are susceptible to witchcraft". It's a wonder what their own mothers thought of this!

The book was printed and went through twenty-nine editions before 1669. It carried the blessing of a papal bull called the *Summis Desiderantes Affectibus*, but although Pope Innocent VIII gave it his blessing, he never put his name to it. Witch hunting had become legal... The witch hunts started in Germany in 1484 and spread to Austria, Switzerland, Hungary, Sweden, France, Spain, England then Scotland.

It would enter England during Queen Elizabeth's reign and six months later Mary Queen of Scots would endorse it in a bill, legalising witch hunts in 1562. In Scotland there would be over 4,000 trials, resulting in around 1,600 deaths. Records are incomplete, as it got so common that actual names in records are casually replaced by "some witches burnt", leaving us with an idea of more than one person being destroyed — but there were many burnings of twenty people at one go!

In Torsåker, Sweden, 71 people, many of whom were children, were executed in a single day in 1675! In the town of Bamberg in Germany, 600 would be executed between the years 1626 and 1631.

My previous book *The Weem Witch* documented the history of the twenty-six witches of Pittenweem. Files containing the actual documents from the year-long trials came my way and I wrote the whole sad story. Largo had at least eleven witches found within its borders, and there is a connection between the Pittenweem witches and the Largo ones.

This is an accurate account of what remains of the Largo witches' story, although the information is scattered. The following is as damning as any other witch hunt.

Witches were blamed for bad harvests, poor fishing, boats lost, ailments and disease, illness in farm animals and general malice.

In Scotland we have this excellent piece on finding witches:

> "Early in the morning on the first Monday of each of the four quarters of the year, the smoke from a witches house goes against the wind, this may be seen by anyone who takes the trouble of rising early and going to an eminence whence the witches house can be seen."
>
> (*Witchcraft and Second Sight* 1902)

In Pittenweem, six miles along the coast from Largo, the Minister of the village was busy interrogating a woman claimed to be a witch. His name was Nichol Dagleish, and he was with the first of twenty-six witches that would be found here. It was the year 1593.

Janet Loquar would be the first name on the slate of the many witches found over these sad years in Pittenween. Of Janet's crime there is no written knowledge, but she would have been subjected to torture to gain her confession. Using the rules in the *Malleus Maleficarum* as a guide to procure a guilty verdict, she would usually be subjected to the pricker, a hellish device with even more hellish logic behind it.

The Devil, when converting victims to his forbidden faith, was believed to take people's baptismal rights from them and give them a mark of his own. If a blemish, being a mole or wart on the skin, couldn't be found as evidence, it followed that it had to lie under the skin, being a spot hidden and insensible to pain. A man would be employed to stick a long pin or spike into the woman or man in various points of the body, to try to find a spot where no blood came out or the witch didn't cry in pain. If at any time the witch confessed, she would be released for a while and then asked the same question again. In that way it became a confession "free from torture". The next step would be the witch's termination.

Janet Loquar was found guilty and she was taken to St Andrews to be was burnt with others.

In 1597 Nichol Dagliesh had excelled himself in his hunt for witches; he found David Zeaman, Jannet Foggow, Beatrix Fergusson, Jannet Williamson and Frite Gunter, all within the Pittenweem boundary.

Of these people David Zeaman was a pedlar selling wares around the doors; not being from the town he aroused suspicion and was arrested. During the torture process more names were mentioned and others would follow; again they were taken to St Andrews and burned outside the castle there in huge fires.

The threat of witchcraft became such a terror to the Largo Presbytery that they issued an appeal to King James VI himself, "to cease travelling around the country as famine and pestilence is affecting the Presbytery, but also of the discoverie of the gryt empire of the devil in this contrey be Witchcraft".

A woman called Margaret Aitkin of Balweary came forward to the church to offer her help in finding witches in the Largo area. Saying she herself was a witch and could find others, she travelled around the country pointing out suspects, but was exposed as a fraud by the end of the year.

In the St Andrews kirk sessions 1582–1600, we read that when King James VI was in St Andrews to evict two troublesome ministers (Black and Wallace), he asked to see the incarcerated witches in person, being five from Pittenweem, and as Dagleish had been in Largo we can presume that Margaret Aitken was in this number.

> "1597, 7th July. Mr Nichol Dagleische proponit that the crounner had cravit of him the extract of the despositions of the witches to be burnt in St Andrews quilk he had grantit be the advice of the session."

The witches were condemned by the king in person and burnt outside St Andrews Castle. Although records reveal that Margaret Aitken was released as a fake, her jailed fellows were not so lucky.

In 1603, Nichol Dagliesh, with his obvious skills for finding witches, was then called to Largo by the ministry to be a guest in an arrest. Janet Small had been arrested on witchcraft charges on 20 October and was asked to appear before the Church elders on 15 December. At the inquest Janet confessed all she was accused of, claiming she had done everything at the direction of another witch called Agnes Anstruther of Dysart (a small village near Kirkcaldy). Agnes was summoned to the court but failed to appear. Her husband appeared and said his wife was too ill to attend.

With Nichol Dagliesh's experienced hands involved in the matter, Janet Small was soon to confess under the torture, with two other women now being dragged into the case. A local man named Alexander Martyne was called as a witness against two sisters called Beatrix and Christian Traillis, who were from the back of Largo in a farming area called Auchendownie, to the west side of Largo Law.

Again what exactly they were accused of is not recorded but a jail would have been needed for the incarceration of the three women and their torture process. Sir John Wood's castle is not 400 metres from the parish church in Largo, and I think this is where their torture would have taken place, as no other information of a "thief's hole" or jail exists in the records about Largo. (Pitcruvie Castle was the seat of the Lyndsay family and their castle is very near to the Auchendownie area of Largo, but my feeling is that both Beatrix and Christian Traillis would have been dealt with nearer to the parish church.)

The outcome is unknown, no record exists of what happened to the three women, but Nichol Dagliesh had processed several to the fires already and there's no reason why he should have stopped short here. In St Andrews that year another burning took place with the sad comment: "some wimmin burnt". So commonplace had the burnings become, that the mention of their actual names became unimportant.

I think the two sisters and Janet Small perished in the flames outside the castle in St Andrews. Agnes Anstruther appears in court records again in 1613 where she was at the St Andrews Presbytery being questioned by the Archbishop; the outcome was not noted.

Another witch is mentioned in the records of St Andrews Parish as coming from Largo in 1644. She's named as Jonet Wylie. Once more the outcome is not noted, but at this date it is mentioned that along the coastline of Fife in the space of one month thirty witches were burned (five in Pittenweem alone).

Another more fortunate person was Thomas Wilson, the schoolmaster in Largo. Accounts of his accusations lie in the Parish records, which state that in "1653 the Presbytery of St Andrews met at Largo Kirk and ordained that Thomas Wilson the school master, should be removed at the following Martinmas, for profainlie taking the name of the devil in his mouth twyse, for tippling and taunting, and for not praying loud enough regularly every morning and evening in the School". Thomas Wilson afterwards stood in front of the pulpit, while the preacher publicly rehearsed his faults, and then the delinquent confessed on his knees that God was righteous, and desired other people to pray for him. He seems to have been forgiven after this show of repentance, for in the Lamont diary (*see* next chapter) it states that he was buried at Largo Kirk between his previous two wives, who had died before him.

Pitcruvie Castle to the north west of Largo, the seat of the Lyndsay family, was once a magnificent structure. It is at least 20 metres high in a standard square box shape, with walls a metre thick. It must have been pretty majestic in its day but it has now fallen to dreadful ruin. One can still see the remains of two vaulted floors and the remains of a circular tower which contained the staircase; another two vaulted chambers lie on the lower ground floor or cellar area which could have been used as a dungeon as the only entrance was a trapdoor from the roof of the ground floor.

The Traillis sisters could have been placed in here after the arrest for witchcraft; there are no records to state otherwise.

Below the castle ruins runs the Kiel Burn, a freshwater stream three to four metres across, where trout, although small, can be caught by fishing line and that is the place where the ladies of Largo used to take their washing and laundry in the 18th century, taking advantage of the clean water and flat area surrounding to hang clothes. A few hundred metres from the castle, if you follow the river, lies a small stone bridge, now hidden in the undergrowth but still of sound structure, known as the fairy bridge. It was so called because witches were supposed to practise their art here in the shadow of the castle by the Kiel Burn. This legend may again spring from the two sisters Christian and Beatrix Traillis who came from Auchendownie, not far from this location. Again the obvious dungeon at the castle may have held the two sisters before being walked to the church for interrogation.

The famous witch Janet Cornfoot was tortured and imprisoned as a witch in Pittenweem, then brutally murdered; she had a relationship with a mariner called Mr White in Pittenweem but she refused to cohabit with him. She got in trouble with the church in Pittenweem who called her before the session to ask why she wouldn't live with Mr White who was a "decent and sober man". She chose to stay with her brother in Largo, who was also dragged up to face the Largo kirk session for openly gambling in his house in 1714. The Cornfoot family also have records of James Cornfoot living in Newburn in 1765 (commissary court of St Andrews 1700–1809).

In all, Largo had at least eleven witch accusations...

Margaret Atkine 1597 ... released, probably banished as a fake

Janet Small, 1603 ... outcome unknown

Beatrix and Christian Traillis ... outcome unknown

Agness Anstruther ... caught in Dysart; two trials; probable termination

Jonet Wylie, 1644 ... outcome unknown but burning of some witches in St Andrews this year in which she may have been burned

Thomas Wilson, 1653 ... released after much penance

Two women from Newburn in Largo ... hanged, then burnt in Cupar, with others before them who before going to execution named the two women condemning them; at least four burnt, 1661 November (*see* Lamont's Diary in the next chapter).

(This could be the Traillis sisters being condemned by Janet Small, but no record exists otherwise.)

Chapter 5

Lamont's Diary

While England's Samuel Pepys (1633–1703), watched and documented from inside London (the Roman town of Londinium) the Civil War, the Dutch War, the Plague and the Great Fire of London unfolded before him as he worked as an English naval administrator and as a Member of Parliament.

Up north in another Lundin (albeit about a thousand times smaller!) there was another diarist, John Lamont of Lundin Castle in Lundin Links, who captured national events in his own diary. He covered the execution of Charles I, the execution of the Duke of Hamilton and Montrose, the plague, deaths and marriages of local lairds, the English occupation of Largo and sex-mad hermaphrodites!

John's brother was chaplain at Lundin Castle, and John had residence there also. He wrote three volumes of diaries of which sadly the third volume is now lost. The first volume (Diary I) was about the years 1649–1663 and was gifted to John Lamont of Largo (his nephew) who was a surgeon. It was left by him at his death to General Durham (of Largo House) and from him to Arniston House library.

Diary II covered the years 1664–1671 and was gifted to James Lumisdaine of Lathallan in Collinsburgh, and then handed down to James Lumsden in 1830.

Diary III was given to James Lumisdain also, but its whereabouts now are a mystery.

Lamont writes in an age where the letter "f" was sometimes used in preference to the letter "s"! When reading this literature it can become very tiresome and confusing, an example of this type of writing is as follows from the Diary

1649 — March 9th

> Duck Hamilton was beheaded att London by the fectaries ther: as also the Earl of Hollande, and the Lord Capell that fame day also. The faid Duke of Hamilton vpon the fcaffold, confeffed that his religion was to the Church of Scotland, that he ever had been loyal to the leate king and wifhed weill to his pofteritie that none more at all tymes defired the peace and happiness of this and the other King, he wifhed his blood, in order to the peace of the kingdom, might be the last spilt.

As you can see from above — the Duke of Hamilton's last speech before his execution — the language is not quite what we are used to reading today and it is hard going. I have taken the liberty of putting the diary articles related to Largo in chronological order and in today's English. I add my own comments now and again. It is quite fantastic that these records still exist and they show how hard life was in 17th-century Largo.

Lamont Diary Book I

1649—September ... The Parish in Largo builds a house for the School master a Mr Thomas Wilson, Mr Magill being Minister.

1650—January ... Robert Maitland the Laird of Lundin Castle made his repentance for having a hand in the late engagement against England. Mr Mcgill minister of Largo did receive him and presently after the Government being read, he did swear the item emitted by the General assembly.

(This engagement was the disaster of the Battle of Preston in August 1648; the Royalist army was surprised by Oliver Cromwell's forces and put to full flight)

1650—March ... Fast at Largo Kirk for the earl of James Graham Montrose.

(The Earl of Montrose had just landed in Scotland from the Orkneys, trying to raise the clans for another assault against Oliver Cromwell. It seems that Largo Parish supported the royalist army)

1650—June ... A disease commonly called the Irish Aygo, was a terrible sore pain of the head, some saying their heads did open! The ordinary remedy was the tying up of the head. A disease not known before this year, known to the inhabitants of the kingdom. It was rife in Largo Parish by the end of the month.

(This was apparently a malaria-type disease with an acute phase, hence the name Aygo or Ague, from the French word for 'acute'.)

1650—July ... the Lord Lorne, the Marquess of Argyle's eldest son, was in Edinburgh Castle, (then under a garrison of Cromwell's roundhead soldiers) the English threw a lead bullet at him (85g weight) the ball struck him in the head in which he lay four hours, he regained and recovered after being trepanned twice.

(What we have here is early brain surgery with no anaesthetic, simply drilling a hole into the skull to release pressure on the brain)

1651—March ... James Robertson, commonly known as the sweet malt man, who dwelt on the north side of Cameron Bridge, was hanged at Kirkcaldy for incest with his little daughter, and called Janet Forman, his wife at the same time being alive. The said Janet before the execution fled and escaped the hands of justice — he was a man in his life time who was a great drunkard and a great swearer.

1651—September ... Scots that went from Stirling to England were routed by Oliver Cromwell and his roundheads near Worcester — the King (Charles II) escaped but the Duke of Hamilton was wounded and died seven days later. The Earl of Rothes was placed in the Tower as 400 officers were taken prisoner among were the Earl of Lundie Castle, six or seven thousand prisoners were taken, English and Scottish, with nine ministers and eighty lieutenants taken.

(The battle was an attempt by Charles II to regain his father's throne. The royal army left Scotland to head to London with the intention of picking up support on the way.

Cromwell's spies had alerted him in advance and he had an army of 31,000 men waiting near Worcester. Charles's army of 16,000 English and Scots fought well, pushing Cromwell's forces from the field, but reinforcements arrived and the battle turned. The Earl of Derby was executed and eight thousand Scots prisoners were sent to Bermuda and the West Indies. With the Earl of Lundie taken, there would be a large contingent of the men folk from Largo involved in this battle and killed or deported!)

1652—July ... A great part of Glasgow was burnt by fire, between the market place and the bridge. It took fire again three or four days after: about a thousand families were burnt. The first fire continued for the space of eighteen hours, the next about twelve hours. Gathering of contributions for relief was done at Largo church.

1652—August ... Some of Major General Dean's regiment of foot soldiers who were now stationed at Largo and Leven were called to challenge and arrest Mr J Magilly, Minister of Largo. He had ended a sermon and finished it by saying a prayer for the prisoners in England (the Earl of Lundie) he said "they suffer for unrighteous sake". They came to quarter some foot soldiers on him who pulled down the stool of repentance, and charged him with praying for the king.

(The "stool of repentance" was an item common to Scottish churches, it was a chair that could be hoisted in the air in front of the parish members as the Minister would berate the victim for whatever sins he had committed. It was a chair of embarrassment that was also commonly known as a "cuttie stool".)

1652—September ... Robert Seaton, one of the ploughmen of Lundin, fled upon a report that he had lain several times with several mares about the meadows of Lundin. His fleeing does confirm the truth of the report, William Millar of Lundin Mill did reveal this at Cupar Court Sept 14 before the English appointed to try such gross faults. He was apprehended in Lothian and taken to Stirling on the 23rd Sept, where he was appointed to suffer. He was finally executed.

(Dear oh dear, a case of gross bestiality in my home town, a mare of all things? Being "appointed to suffer" seems to me like a fair bit of torture was given before he was finally hung or beheaded.)

1652—Aug ... the laird of Lundin castle (being prisoner of war in the Tower of London) came down post from London, he has been given a pass from Oliver Cromwell to come home for three months after paying a deposit of fifty pounds sterling. Released 30 August– November 30.

1653—February ... A great sea battle between England and Holland with much men o' war sunk and merchant ships.

1653—February ... A hermaphrodite was taken from Lundin and hanged in Edinburgh. Because he was unclean and had lain with several men's wives in the area, he was both man and woman; he was a thing not ordinary in this kingdom! His custom was always to go in woman's habit.

(This is another astonishing piece of history, "because he was unclean" suggests he may have had a sexually transmitted disease, or the villagers just found his behaviour too much to handle. It seems he was a massive hit with the ladies though, but to declare he was "not ordinary in this kingdom" shows the utter disgust of the locals, or then again maybe just jealousy that someone so unusual could be such a charmer with the girls.)

1653—March ... David Lundie (from Lundie castle) being at Cupar on the market day, was put in the thieves' hole because he was found drunk by the English soldiers there. He stayed in the place from ten o'clock till one next afternoon.

1653—March ... About the middle of the month the English forces' horse and foot that lay in the shire of Fife betook themselves to the fields and several parishes were demanded to provide coals for them, Largo Parish sent thirty loads.

(The English occupation had to be fed and looked after, with all parishes providing for the soldiers. With the loss in menfolk during the previous war, parishes in Fife began to feel the strain of the extra expense, as we shall see)

1653—August 6 ... there came further orders to Largo Parish to provide for fifty loads of coals to Struther park, coals were sent Aug 9th, again a further demand was made for sixty-six loads of coals for the English stationed at Falkland.

1653—August ... Before the middle of the month the English caused to make a public proclamation at Edinburgh, that none whatsoever should pray for the King any more, either in church or with family through the nation. Notice fixed on all church doors, that no one can pretend ignorance.

1653—August 21 ... Being the Sabbath Mr J Magill preached at Largo, where there was a collection after the sermon was ended for some Prisoners at Tinmouth, taken at Dunbar 1651 by the English.

(The River Tyne has its mouth just to the west of Dunbar.)

1653—December ... About ten days before the month ended, Thomas Peatson a servant at Lundie place with William Spence and Robert Braith, dwellers in the Overmorton of Lundie and two ploughmen were collecting limestones in the quarry at Thomas ford beside Hatton. While they were working they fell upon the bones of a dead body that had been put there (by all appearance with no honest dealing) the bones were rotten, the person maybe fourteen or fifteen years old.

Henderson the good man of Hatton is now dead but memory states he had a servant not above fifteen years as a travelling boy (for the bones were not of someone who had come of great age); he must have struck him and he lay there. If this be the body of the boy I will bring it up at the next session. However Andrew Henderson, his son now dwelling nearby, came and saw the bones and deferred to have the same men who found them to cover them again in earth. In the same quarry they did accordingly.

(Here, it seems, we have a murder. The quarry I think is further up the main road from Wood's tower. A beautiful house stands there, with excellent views over the Largo bay. In my youth it belonged to the Forgan family, the two boys

Mike and Brian and I myself used to play in the old quarry in the woods next to the house; it had obviously not been in use for a long time, but was deep enough to show — as I remember — it had been mined extensively.)

1654—March 24th ... a party of English horsemen in Buckhaven shot and wounded a Mr John Mitchel, an inhabitant there, and within an hour he died.

(At this time the English were recruiting horses for the soldiers stationed in the local areas, more than fifty horses were taken in the Largo area alone, no one was spared this theft as the minister lost three. But local tensions towards the occupying troops rose as we will see in the following texts.)

1654—March ... The Laird of Lundin Castle came home to Lundin. This was his second time back since capture at Worcester.

1654—April ... Old Robert Duncan departed out of this life and was interred in the Church of Largo April 17. He was the age of ninety-three and was the oldest man in the Parish of Largo.

1654—May 11 ... Being Friday six o'clock at night in Lundin Links, a party of English was passing when two of Kenmore's men charged the front two men and shot one of the horses. The two Kenmore's retired with the English in pursuit but they could not catch them. The English went to Newburn and found some of Kenmore's men, (these were Robert the 4th Viscount of Kenmore's men, a great favourite of Charles I) they surprised them and wounded five of them and took as many again as prisoners. They shot

David Mitchells in the knee and wounded a woman in the leg with the same bullet. They also struck Margaret Bennet, Andrew's daughter. They went to Lundie Castle with the prisoners; nine went to the English camp at Burntisland then Edinburgh. One prisoner was so badly wounded in his left side he had to stay at Lundie where he died. The woman who was shot in the leg had to have it cut from her by a surgeon from Kirkcaldy.

(A shocking piece of rebellious nature, from the local disbanded remains of the Scottish army. With the constant demands for horses, food and coal, and the general brutality from the occupying forces, it was not long before other such instances occurred)

1654—At the Mercat Cross in Edinburgh a proclamation was raised to show pardons to the eminent men involved in the recent wars in England. All parties shown here must pay fines to the Protector Oliver Cromwell. Non-payment will result in confiscated property.

David Leslie of St Monance ... £4,000
Laird of Lundie Castle ... £1,000
Laird of Anstruther ... £1,000

(The list of prisoners obliged to pay for their liberty is huge, and so I have only put the ones living near to Largo.)

1654—April ... Three horses were taken from Largo Parish by the English, two from Lundie and another two from Newburn.

1654—May ... Being the Sabbath at night several prisoners being at Edinburgh Castle escaped over the walls using blankets as ropes. Lord Kinnoull, Lieutenant colonel Marshall, the laird of Lughtton, George Mountgomerie escaped. Two English went over the wall (both were killed in the breakout), the sentry and the castle keeper. George Mountgomerie fell and with sore injuries died later.

1654—July 20 ... David Young, a servant in the castle of Lundie, was helping others in the ground to carry and transport some beer to Kirkcaldy, and in returning they stopped at Dysart and drank liberally so that the said David did have several falls from his horse he rode upon. By length he could not sit on horseback, his other carriers left him by the way in a place called Heart of Law, a place near Wemyss, a little west of Cameron Bridge, thinking when awoken he would make his way back home to Lundin Links. But he did not appear next day or the next. His wife went in search of him and found him dead! He was buried at Wemyss church, being the one nearest to the body.

1654—May ... Bridge put up over Lundin mill burn, timbers brought from Largo for construction of a bridge, contributions from all at Largo parish from the Minister James McGill and some elders.

1655—January ... There comes from the English garrison at Falkland a demand for 52 loads of coal.

Feburary ... 26 loads ...

March ... 26 loads ...

April ... 20 loads ...

May ... 20 loads.

(An interesting note here is that it was now one hundred years to the month since Mary Queen of Scots visited Lundin Castle. She was going to Edinburgh from St Andrews with some dignitaries and mounted troops when she stopped in at Lundin Castle.

The information about this visit comes from a man named Randolph who was the English Queen Elizabeth's Ambassador to the Scottish court.

He writes "at her coming to the Laird of Lundie's house in Fife, who is a grave and ancient man, with white beard. He kneeleth down unto her, and saith like words like these:— 'Madame this is your house and the land belongeth to the same; all my goods and gear is yours. These seven boys (his sons) will wear our bodies in your grace's service without your majesties charge, and we will serve you truly. But Madam, one humble petition I would make unto your grace, in recompense of this — that your Majesty will have no mass in this house so long as it pleaseth your grace to tarry in it.'

"The Queen Mary asked 'why?'

"He replied 'I know it to be worse than the Mickle Devil, and worse spiteful words against it'."

The Queen, feeling very insulted, went back to St Andrews and immediately sent a troop of horse to the laird of Lundie's castle, there they found the old man in his bed at midnight. He was arrested and taken to St Andrews Castle and committed to the prison there. John Knox the reformer and great antagonist of Queen Mary wrote about this unruly treatment of the Laird of Lundie: "this manner of handling and usage being unkind and strange was heavily spoke of among her subjects, it brought a great terror to others who thought themselves warned of greater severity to come from the Queen".

How long was the laird's stay in the bottle dungeon in St Andrews castle is not recorded, but Walter Lundin was still alive in 1572, and recorded by the Edinburgh Parliament as being over ninety years of age.)

1655—August 2nd ... Jean Lyndsay wife to David Achmoutie departed out of this life, she died of purple fever. The first pain she had was a pain in the ear, died 3rd August.

(This "Purple fever" could be what we know as puerperal fever, it was for several centuries the most common type of maternal death following childbirth. It reached epidemic proportions in Europe in early 19th century, caused by bacteria such as streptococcus pyogenes. Basically it was unclean conditions during childbirth. In the Lamont diary many families lose members of this disease; I have omitted many cases to avoid repetition.)

1655—August, all this month for the most part was great rains, but at the end of the month the rains increased greatly. At Lundie mill the water entered the mill door and ran over the head of the bridge, ran away some of the stepping stones at Nether Largo, all done by the violence of the rain water.

*

(We skip a year as nothing of note happens, bar a few nobles from Edinburgh pass away)

1657—the masons begin to build a stone dyke about the church of Kirktown of Largo by the expense of John Wood at cost £50 sterling.

(John Wood was Sir Andrew Wood's relation)

1658—January ... Mr Craw a member of the parish fell in fornication with a woman from the parish, being found with child, but being demanded the question, he answered he could not tell if he was the father of the child. Whereupon he left his charge and fled. His whereabouts are uncertain.

1658—September ... Great floods. Two young laddies drown at Lundie Mill between Hatton and Lundie, both interred at Largo church.

1660—April ... Parliament in England sits and sends a recall to Charles II to come and be their King, he lands at Dover May 29.

1661—John Wood's corpse lands by boat at Elie, it was brought from London, the body was interred in Largo Church.

1661—June 1st ... Mr James Guthrie minister of Stirling was publicly hanged for treason for adhering to the remonstrance "The Causes of God's Wrath". His head was put upon a spike above the Nether Bow. Likewise William Govan, a Scottish officer, was hung for having a hand in the late Majesty's death; he was even said to be the actual man who beheaded him (King Charles I).

(How the tables turn, with Oliver Cromwell's death in 1658 of a malaria-type disease in Whitehall, London. Once

Charles II was reinstated to the monarchy, in 1661, 30 January, exactly twelve years since Charles I was executed, Cromwell's body was dug out its grave and hung in a gibbet at Tyburn, London. Now the Roundheads who put such demands on Largo Parish were disbanded and the officers were hiding from Charles's retribution.)

1661—August ... The lord Cranston, Earl of Leven's son-in-law, in way of duel killed Captain Scrymgeour, Earl of Dundee's brother.

1661—November ... this month the two women in Newburn that were apprehended about a year ago for burning Mr Lawrence Oliphatt's house, were hanged at Cupar in Fife. Being found guilty by the Judge, also they were accused of witchcraft, because dilated by some of their own neighbours in the town who were themselves burnt a little before this execution. The women did confess neither crime but still pleaded innocence of burning the house and witchcraft before their own execution. Mr Allen Colvill justice deputy was present at the sentence as Judge.

(Accused by neighbours who themselves were burnt for witchcraft; it's a sad situation that this was repeated all over Scotland. The sadness to me is, again, no names are given for the victims. They are not registered in any Scottish records of witch trials ... just casually named as "some witches"! In the case of the two mentioned above with others who accused them before they were burned themselves ... at least four unnamed witches from Largo)

1662—January ... Lundie Mill took fire and was badly burnt, Largo Parish lost eleven bags of oats in the fire.

1662—July ... Between seven and eight in the morning at Lundie, John Rattay one of the plough men being in the garden yard cutting trees on the North Dyke for the brew house, Alex Cunningham, elder, in Lundie mill, came in to the yard and stood a little under where James was cutting. James cried out beware as the tree fell. Alex was immediately smitten, he was buried in Largo church on the 24th July.

(Nothing more than a tragic accident, but reading an account from an 1830 document when the tower was owned by Mr Gilmour of Montrave, when visitors walked up the Lundie Castle staircase a bloodied spot would be pointed out on one of the floors where someone bled out. It was said no washing would get the bloodstains of the floor, so it was eventually boarded over.)

1663—August ... Leper William Sandelen's wife departed in St Andrews out of this life and was interred the day she died. She was unwell a month before her death or more, it was constantly confirmed to be the French pox she died of.

(The French pox was syphilis)

In the time of sickness Mr J Wood came to visit her and she confessed to him that Thomas Moncrieff, brother-in-law to Archbishop Sharp of St Andrews, gave her the disease, by lying with her three or four times. He says he has had no meddling with her at all; others say she had lain with three other men besides her husband; others name eleven more!

(Archbishop Sharp was to be assassinated on Magnus Moor near St Andrews by Covenanters in 1679.)

From 1663–64 ... pages are ruined by rodent and damp action.

Lamont Diary Book II

1664—December ... this month a comet in the sky did appear about eight o'clock in the morning: it was very terrible in its first appearance. In the evening it was like a candle blowing out. It appeared all through December.

1665—April ... A hospital was built at Largo by the deceased John Wood's money. Built of stone by a master mason Robert Wolf from Edinburgh and some local men he hired for the work (eighteen to twenty men). It was built for 9,000 merks with 100 more if the building was built well. It has three roofs and fourteen rooms with a public hall; each room has a bed and a closet. When it is finished about six people will live here.

(John was a descendant of Sir Admiral Wood)

1665—April ... About January came great snow storms, leaving much snow and fierce frost. Nearly two hundred sheep died in the fields in Fife, including Lundie, but it was fine by April 1st.

1656—May ... James Henderson, servant to Bessie Barclay in Largo, perished in Leven's waters on horseback. The tides were full in, some women forbade him to take a short cut. Next day his corpse was found among the rocks. His body was interred in Methil parish. The rains were such that old Lady Lundie, Katherine Lindsay, who had lived here some thirty-eight years, said she had never seen the like.

1665—June ... A fast appointed to be kept in Scotland for repentance to the land and success to his Majesty's fleet against the Hollanders. The two fleets met and the Dutch were worsted, losing 24 vessels burnt, 9,000 men killed. Only one British vessel lost, the *Charitie*, and 400 men killed.

1665—September ... Wednesday, A fast appointed by the council in Edinburgh to be kept throughout the whole kingdom on behalf of the city of London in England and other parts of the country now suffering under the weighty hand of God by the plague of pestilence. In London five thousand a week were dying, by end of September it was seven to eight thousand.

(The Black Death had in the past wiped out one third of the population of Europe. Now the Great Plague struck London.

Spread by rats, it was aboard ships that docked at ports and it wouldn't be long before St Andrews and Leith would feel the effects of this contagious deadly disease, brought from ships from London and Europe. The plague could strike a man dead in four hours.

Daniel Defoe wrote about six friends laughing from a pub in Shoreditch in London as a man they knew and hated went by in a hearse full of dead plague victims. Some even owed the man money, and found it very amusing as his body went past; by next day all but one would be dead; the survivor watched all his friends go past in the cart to the plague pits. All were taken by the pestilence. Through the Lamont diaries every so often a man of noble birth will die, or maybe his wife. It's about once every eight pages or so but not worth including here as it carries no real interest. From the above statement about the plague we now see in the Diary a vast dictation of recently deceased people, no reason for death is given but it's obvious the plague has reached this area and is reaping havoc. I list some names of the dead.)

1656—newly deceased ... Laird of Buchaly, the Archbishop of St Andrews' wife, Doctor David Balfour, Alex Martin, Old Laird of Lathone, Arditt Douglas, Doctor John Colvill, David Balfour's Mother (in Drumeldrie in Lundin Links) and Andrew Wilson.

(The list goes on but the reader can grasp that the plague is in the area, as you can see it has taken its toll on doctors, obviously called out to sick patients with the plague who pass the disease on. Dr David Balfour has passed the disease on to his unfortunate mother, who sadly died. In St Andrews, where the plague arrived in the town in boats from the continent and England, it is noticeable that a huge number of priests and doctors were struck down by the pestilence. They came into close contact with the diseased victims when giving aid or delivering the last rites. Walter Bower, one of the main authors of the *Scotichronicon*, a series of sixteen books documenting early Scottish history, records that at least twenty-four of the priests in St Andrews church, about a third of the number there, died within a short period of the plague's arrival. In England it is recorded that at least forty-five percent of ministers and priests were slain by the pestilence.

In Largo graveyard up from North Feus across from today's primary school, there is a flat piece of land in the middle of the graves, an area of bare grass with a huge monkey-puzzle tree in the middle, a huge umbrella over what was the resting place of the poor and of plague victims. The plague killed so many that there were not enough to bury the dead. Bodies due to the high rate of infection had to be got rid of as quickly as possible, so communal pits were the norm, some with thousands of bodies all in one pit. The infestation of the pestilence across the country was dealt with primitively. The speed and quickness of death was astonishing. There is a theory of rats spreading the disease through infected fleas, the fleas biting humans and spreading the disease through infected blood. But scientists still excavate plague burials for evidence to support the rat theory. It is an open question whether this disease was similar to today's Ebola virus that occasionally terrorises African countries. Its speed and fatality does not suggest the slow spread of rats.

With prayers having no effect on the disease, our ancestors in desperation looked to supernatural methods to prevent infection. Along the coast in Fife, villagers put loaves of fresh bread on poles in the graveyard areas, the bread eventually going hard and mouldy showing blue and purple mould, a similar colour to the plague victim's skin; their vain hope was that the plague was attacking the bread rather than them. It would be carefully dropped to the ground where it could be buried and never disturbed. They believed "that the discolouration of the loaves showed the veritable presence of the pestilence, which save for this antidote, would have spread death and ruin amongst the inhabitants." *Fifiana*, Conolly, 1869, p117)

1666—The Laird of Largo Mr Francis Durham was accountable to collection from creditors at Edinburgh.

(The Durhams built a huge mansion in Largo in 1750 "Largo House". It was used by Polish forces in the Second World War, and stood till 1951, when the owners had the roof removed. It is now a total ruin. My father as a boy in Largo was invited to a party at the house before its problems and can remember the place as grand and spacious. I myself spent most of my childhood climbing the ruins and exploring what was left of the ruin, great fun!)

1666—May ... Being the day of the races at Cupar Fife, it was watched by the Majesty's commissioner the Earl of Rothes. For a while his horse did carry the prize being a great cup of silver. Mr Stobbs' horse was second and Lord Montgomery's horse last, being three in the race.

Lord Lithgow and Lord Carnegie passed some unkind words in which they drew off towards Tarvet Broom and drew swords on one another. Lord Carnegie gave Lord Lithgow a sore wound, others did ride between the duelling men and two horses were thrust through and both died. Both men were arrested and put in Cupar jail by his Majesty's commissioner.

1667—January 24th ... Captain William Garstairs appeared at Billy Barclay's house in Lundin Links where a fight broke out. Billy was shot in the leg by Captain William, the reason being that some months earlier, Billy cut hairs from Captain William Garstairs' horse's tail. Captain Garstairs called and demanded satisfaction, where a fight ensured.

1667—April ... being the Sabbath. The sentence of excommunication was read out at the Church of Largo by John Auchinleck minister, against David Dickson and Marion Gibb his wife's sister for laying in incest one with another. The scandal was delivered at the parish and both were seen fleeing from the discipline of the church and remaining obstinate in their sin.

1667—December ... being a great tempest of wind snow and rain, there was an English vessel about the Isle of May that suffered the violence of the storm so that a boat was lowered and the crew made their escape. The crew all seven of them landed on Largo beach at Johnstone's Mill, and after landing one of the men took ill and died. They interred his corpse on the land behind the mill. Next day the beach of Largo and Buckhaven was full of pieces of broken vessel.

(The body buried here could be the one the railway workers in 1856 found when digging and building the railway tracks. That skeleton, it was reported, once it was disturbed, fell to dust. Compared with the Pict skeletons that had been prepared and buried in the sands, it seems that earthen burial decayed the bones of the skeleton much faster with the acidity of the soil)

1670—April ... One Major Weir, who lived in Edinburgh, who had some allowance from the town council, being an old man aged seventy-five or seventy-six, was burnt at the Gallowlee between Leith and Edinburgh for incest with his sister. He confessed to bestiality in laying with beasts and laying with his sister since she was sixteen.

He would not suffer the ministers to pray for him, neither would he take God's mercy. When forced to take it he said, "And now what better am I?" Jean Weir being about sixty was hanged at Edinburgh. She confessed to incest and practising witchcraft, on the gallows she had no arms tied and smote the executioner on the cheek.

They both died impenitent persons.

The Lamont Diary tails off till 1671 with the usual marriages and deaths, not anything of note to put in here. The third volume that would have carried on from here has been lost.

Chapter 6

What Shall We Do with a Drunken Sailor?

In August 2008, Dr David Caldwell, a member of the National Museum of Scotland, led a dig on an island 750 kilometres off the Chilean coast — the island of Aguas Buenas or Juan Fernandez.

After examining the island he found what he was looking for, an old encampment showing traces of a European settler's stay. Post holes showed where a shelter once stood. Another close by was near a fresh water stream and had a view over the island's natural harbour, in fact a great viewpoint for someone looking into the horizon ... someone watching, hoping. Someone who would stand here on this viewpoint and wait four years and four months till sails appeared over the horizon and finally a rescue became a reality. This man would be written down in legend as Robinson Crusoe; his real name was Alexander Selkirk, a Scotsman from the village of Largo.

Alexander was born in Lower Largo in 1676. There is little to tell of his youth, but his father was a shoemaker with a house just up from the shore from Largo beach, his mother was called Eupham Mackie and he was one of seven brothers.

His legend starts in Upper Largo church, where the wrath of the minister's "cuttie stool" awaited one Alexander Selkirk for a breach of the peace offence.

The Minister John Auchinleck's session records from Upper Largo Church explain the details as follows:

1695—Alexander Selchraig to be summoned August 25, this same day the session mett, the qlk day Alexander Selchraig son of John Selchraig elder in Nether Largo was dilated for his undecent beaiver in ye church; the church officer is ordirred to ga and cite him to compeer befoor our session agst ye nixt dyett. August 27th, ye session mett, Alexander did not compeer. The glk day Alexander Selchraig, son of John Selchraig elder, called but did not compeer being gone away to ye seas; this business is to be continued till his return.

Alexander had come home from a fishing trip and gone into his father's house in Lower Largo where his brother offered him a drink. Alex took a cup of water from his brother, said his thanks and had a good mouthful, but it was a joke! The cup was seawater. Alex spat the contents over the floor and took serious offence to his brother's laughter. A fight started, fists flew between the brothers. His father John threw himself into the mêlée and tried to separate the warring sons, but the battle spilled outside where it became a community spectacle. Another brother and then his wife then got involved. The fight was eventually broken up!

The end result was a report to the Parish for his violent behaviour, in which he was called to the session for punishment (basically a charge of assault), but before the day in front of the clergy came, he hopped aboard the first sailing vessel in the harbour and was off for a career at sea.

Nowadays only one or two small crab boats use the harbour's facilities and to see the small boats in the harbour today it's hard to imagine a busy fishing fleet in existence but that Largo was a fishing port is no exaggeration. The fishing community around this Fife coast were the most superstitious and untrusting of people, with mortality high among the crews. Lucky charms and significant signs ruled whether you would actually go to sea or not. In the 1800s those traditions still prevailed in nearby harbours such as Anstruther and Pittenweem.

It was seen as unlucky to mention salmon, partridges, pigs. To see a rabbit, hare or seal was to see the fishing abandoned. It was unlucky to meet an old woman en route to the boat, or a minister. Meeting any of the above en route to your vessel would render the voyage cursed and the boatmen would not risk the day.

Belle Patrick wrote in 1960 in her book *Recollections of East Fife Fisher Folk* about her father's boat in Anstruther at the beginning of the 20th century. When a young minister came for a visit to the town, and walked to the harbour to introduce himself to the crowd of fishermen on the boat front, he was welcomed by stony silence and all the fishermen and their wives packed up and went home muttering, leaving the bemused minister standing on his own. He had jinxed the trip and all just left the fishing for another day.

Alexander did return from his sea voyage. He had been aboard a merchant boat, had learned to be an accomplished navigator and had a natural gift for the sea. He returned home to see his parents in 1701, only to find that he had a pressing engagement with a certain "cuttie stool" in Largo church. They had not forgotten his previous stay in Largo. The church records show the session that followed ...

1701 November 25th the session mett, John Selchraige was called and compared, and being examined what was the occasion of the tumult that was in his house, he said he knew not, but that Andrew Selchraige having brought in a canfull of salt water to give his brother Alex. He did take a drink from the can by mistake and his brother did laugh at him for it, his brother Alex did came and beat upon his brother, he run out the house and called his brother. John Selchraige stood betwixt his sons as Alex Selchraige was seeking to get his pistol; John Selkirk [another brother] was compared to appear at the church session and give his statement as he was in the house also ... He declared "he was called by his brother [Andrew] into the house, he came to it and when he entered the house, his mother ran out, he seeing his father sitting on the floor, with his back against the door, he was much troubled, and offered to help him up, and brang him to the fire, at which time he did see his brother, Alexander in the other end of the house casting of his coate, and coming towards him, whereupon his father did get betwixt them, but he knew not what they did as his head was born down by his brother Alexander. But afterwards being liberated by his wife did make his escape. Margaret Bell did compare and enquired to the session that the occasion of the tumult which fell out in her father in law's house in the 7th November;

she said that Alexander Selchraige came running for her husband, John and desiring him to go to his father's house, which he doing, she said she found Alexander gripping both his father and his brother her husband, and she labouring to loose Alex's hands from her husband's head and breast, her husband fled out of doors and she followed him, she cried to the house "you fols loun will you murder your father and my husband both" where upon he followed her to the door, but whether he beat her or not she was in great confusion, she could not distinctly tell, but ever since she hath a sore pain in the head.

Finally the brawler Alexander Selkirk appeared himself before the committee and it seems he stood in a huff during the session, which records "Andrew Selchraige compeared but said nothing to purpose in the foresaid business".

But a further inquiry was demanded by the church, not satisfied by Andrew's attitude. He was demanded again in front of the church session on the 29th November. He was asked to appear before the council, being in presence of the Minister, John Lundine of Baldastard, Magnus Wilson, James Beat, James Smith, William Beat, John Guthrie, James Smith, Thomas Ness, Thomas Morton, William Jerves.

After prayer, Alexander Selchraige was brought forward for his "scandalous contention and disagreeing with his brothers", he said he confessed to drinking a salt water drink, his brother Andrew laughing at him he did beat him twice with a staff; he confessed also that he had spoken very ill words concerning his brothers, and particularly he challenged his elder brother, John to a combat, as he called it.

The session declared that he was to appear before the church congregation and the cuttie stool, and he did so next day when he was addressed before the village and was rebuked and in the strength of the Lord was dismissed. In 1703, Alexander was back at sea and employed upon a boat called the *Cinque Ports* (this was the collective name of the English ports of Sandwich, Dover, Romney, Hastings and Hythe: they were so named after the Norman invasion of 1066 when they were strengthened for French trade).

He was bound for a voyage to the South Seas on duty around the South American coast. The *Cinque Ports* was an armed ship with sixteen guns; the mission was to attack Spanish ships and pirates, relieving the enemy of any riches they carried.

With his navigational experience, he made himself useful on board, so useful he was promoted to "sailing master" under a Mr Charles Pickering, the captain being William Dampier.

He signed on as Alexander Selkirk, not Selchraige. The reason for this is unknown but perhaps it had something to do with his parish problems. He would keep the name for evermore.

Sailing around Argentina in 1704, Mr Pickering became unwell with fever, he eventually died and his position was taken over by a cocky young 21-year-old upstart called Thomas Stradling. Alexander was 28 years old and much more experienced in seafaring than his new master; it brought conflict between the two. The temper of Selkirk that had shown itself in Largo arose again between him and both Captain Dampier and his new senior officer Thomas Stradling. The boat's hull, according to Alexander, was rotten through with worms, they were eating the structure. It needed urgent attention and there was now a 24-hour crew working on the pumps just baling water from the hold. Alexander demanded the ship should be berthed in dry dock to resolve the problem or the ship would surely suffer more damage. With water sloshing around as the pump men tried in vain to stem the leaks, bunks, walls, food and clothes became saturated with the moisture; it must have been horrible conditions to live in, and with so many crew packed below tempers were flaring. The Captain saw no need to alter his journey, but Alex was most persistent, and it was unsettling the crew also. The meat was tainted, bread and biscuit was moving in weevils, the food was inedible, and several of the crew were showing the telltale signs of scurvy. Matters persisted until it came to blows; Alexander demanded to be set ashore on the nearest island, and his captain was only too happy to grant his wish.

The first island in view was Juan Fernandez, consisting of three main volcanic land masses about 460 square kilometres in area.

A boat was lowered with Selkirk's belongings contained in a wooden chest, inside was a Bible, gunpowder, pistol, clothes and his navigational equipment. He was rowed ashore and as the boat set off and its sails disappeared into the horizon, he fully expected to board another ship within the week. Little did he know that four years and four months would pass before he would speak to another soul.

He soon found a supply of fresh water on the island. There were fruit and peppers growing aplenty, and there was a herd of goats running wild. Before long he had a basic camp made with two roofs made from trees. He adapted to his surroundings, captured goats and began farming their milk and meat, and eventually their skins for clothes. It was a terribly lonely existence, however he certainly made the most of what was on offer. But on the seaward horizon, he watched for signs of a ship day after day. Weeks turned to months and the horizon never showed any sails of a boat, any hope of rescue. Years went by in a solitary existence, windswept and bitterly isolated.

Unknown to Alexander, his ship the *Cinque Ports* had travelled 150 kilometres further up the coast, nearly as far as Colombia, but then the worm-ridden timbers about which Alexander had bitterly complained had caved in, just as he had predicted.

The Pacific Ocean flooded in before any maintenance could be brought into effect, the timbers so rotten that the breech in the hull was fatal for the ship. The *Cinque Ports* went down with most of its crew and all its cargo. Barely a handful escaped to the beaches of Colombia, where the occupying Spanish were waiting to capture the survivors including Captain Dampier.

They would be marched to Lima prison in Peru. Therefore, unknown to anyone, Alexander Selkirk was marooned on an island, with his captain in a Spanish jail. There was nobody to tell of the man left on the island and there would be no rescue for four years and four months.

In February 1709, from Alexander's viewpoint high up on the island, finally he saw the unmistakable sight of sails on the horizon. It was two ships, the *Duke* and the *Duchess*, one 350 tonnes, the other 260. Both were men o' war, frigates both armed with thirty-six cannon, on a mission to harass Spanish shipping up the coast.

Captain Woodes Rogers had needed fresh water and sent a crew on land to renew provisions. When they touched down by boat on the beach this hairy, tall, bearded man leapt into view screaming and shouting, wearing goatskin as clothes as he jumped up and down on the beach. Captain Woodes commanded the larger ship, *Duke*, but the master on board the *Duchess* couldn't believe what he was seeing and hearing. He recognised the Scottish accent! But not the man underneath all the hair and beard ... this captain's name was William Dampier! He was Alexander's captain on the *Cinque Ports*, the very man who had marooned him over four years before! What a coincidence!

What was said between the pair is not recorded. Captain Woodes Rogers was an English privateer who would go on to become Governor of the Bahamas and a key figure in suppressing the pirates in the Caribbean. The Spanish called him a pirate as he attacked Spanish vessels. His greatest prize was a Spanish treasure galleon, *Nuestra Señora de la Encarnación y Desengaño*, which he captured off the coast of Mexico later that year. The crew and cargo amounted to two million dollars. More ships added to his growing tally.

Captain Rogers took Alexander Selkirk on board as a mate, and as he showed his fighting ability and had lost none of his navigation qualities, he was soon given one of the Spanish prize ships to command.

Captain Rogers would befriend Alexander, listening to his adventures. He wrote his story in 1712, called "*A Cruising Voyage Round the World: First to the South-Sea, Thence to the East Indies, and Homewards by the Cape of Good Hope* ... contains a journal of all the remarkable transactions ... An account of Alexander Selkirk's living alone four years and four months on an island."

This lengthily titled book would introduce Selkirk to the English-speaking world, and two men from London would take great interest in this strange man from Largo and dress up his story and turn it into literary legend.

Alexander Selkirk was marooned on the island September 4th 1704; he was rescued in February 1709. He was two years in action with Captain Rogers before getting back to Britain in October 1711. In London several of Rogers's friends and acquaintances were introduced to Alexander in the taverns of Wapping, listening eagerly to the fantastic story of this man who lived alone with goats for over four years. Two of these men were unknown authors, Daniel Defoe (1660–1731) and Jonathan Swift (1667–1745). With Captain Rogers's written account to hand they eventually wrote two works of fiction inspired by Alexander Selkirk's story ... these two books would be entitled *Robinson Crusoe* (1719) and *Gulliver's Travels* (1726).

Alexander would spend his next nine years back in Largo; he left with nothing, but arrived back with his share of the prize money with Captain Woodes Rogers being £800, which was a huge sum of money, considering that a labourer was earning one penny a day toiling in the fields.

Alexander stayed in Largo for the next few years and was to miss out on Captain Rogers's most famous moment in his ship the *Pearl*, a battle at sea with the notorious pirate Blackbeard! Blackbeard's real name was Edward Teach. Born in Bristol, he had become a legend in piracy along the Virginian coast of America, which he had terrorised.

His ship grounded on a sandbank, and Blackbeard (so called for his beard wrapped in fuses — they burned as he fought, giving a very scary appearance) was shot with five pistol wounds and cut down by two cutlass wounds before he was beheaded by a Scottish seaman with a claymore. Lieutenant Robert Maynard, who fought the pirate, took full credit for the kill, though!

Back in Largo, Alexander had a church court session to deal with, one in which the ministry had waited six years to have their say, and when that ordeal was dealt with, he had the problem of dealing with being a celebrity of the day. He was pestered wherever he went. *Robinson Crusoe* sold in its thousands to go on to be a bestseller.

His four-year solitude had left him loath to put up with the attention he now attracted. He hated the sound of the human voice and so he left the village to build a camp in Kiel's Den wood away from the village. Although he did have a wife in the village he soon left to go back to sea.

He was signed aboard a boat called the *Weymouth* bound for East Africa, but on this voyage after a few months out, yellow fever and typhoid were claiming three to four lives a day on board. On the 13th of December 1721 the ship's log records that three Englishmen died from disease, one at 8pm, whose name was recorded as Alexander Selkirk.

His body with the two others was cast into the sea, off the Gold Coast.

With his death announced, his wife in Largo (he married in 1717) settled into the family home. Selkirk had hardly been around when he was alive, so with his death life in his household carried on as usual with just a little grieving. But then another woman turned up in Largo at the Selkirk household, and she had a marriage certificate! She was Alexander's wife from Bristol, married some years before 1717! A legal battle was settled in the first wife's favour. She was entitled to have the house and belongings, and the Scottish wife had to leave.

William Cowper wrote a poem about Alexander Selkirk, from the castaway's point of view.

The Solitude of Alexander Selkirk

I am monarch of all I survey,
   My right there is none to dispute;
From the centre all round to the sea,
   I am lord of the fowl and the brute.
O solitude! Where are the charms
   That sages have seen in thy face?
Better dwell in the midst of alarms
   Than reign in this horrible place.

I am out of humanity's reach,
   I must finish my journey alone,
Never hear the sweet music of speech;
   I start at the sound of my own.
The beasts, that roam over the plain,
   My form with indifference see;
They are so unacquainted with man,
   Their tameness is shocking to me.

(and there are five more verses.)

Today in Largo he is still (and I think unfairly) our most famous son. In Upper Largo, the parish church sits a good ten feet higher than the road surrounding it. The church has a circumference wall built by money from Admiral Sir Andrew Wood's relation John Wood in 1657 (£50 was donated towards the construction of the wall). There are several flat gravestones around the church. To the left-hand side as you enter the churchyard, a grave sits alone — a bed of sea shells around it makes it different from the rest. It bears the names of John Selchraige and Euphame Mackie, Andrew Selkirk's mum and dad.

In Lower Largo there is a memorial to Selkirk. His statue stands dressed in goatskin along the Lower Largo main street where his father's house was. The original house was torn down in 1865. There is still a drawing of what the original house once looked like.

The statue has him standing with his hand shielding his eyes in a pose looking over the

14 The Robinson Crusoe statue in Lower Largo

15 A drawing of the original home of Alexander Selkirk. It was replaced by a new building in 1865, on which his statue now stands.

horizon, still looking for the sight of a sail to rescue him from his island, but in hindsight I feel the island was truly his only real home.

When I lived in London I used to travel by bus to and from work in the city. Once when I was on a journey on the 43 bus from London Bridge to Archway, the bus stopped near Old Street next to an old cemetery — there on the graveyard wall was a plaque.

Outside the main gate it gave names of some of the notable occupants of the cemetery. I have a fondness for graveyards and studied the list of privileged notables laid to rest here. One name half-way down the list I knew straight away: it said in bold capitals, Daniel Defoe.

I got off the bus to explore this last resting place of the man who wrote *Robinson Crusoe*. I was interested in what sort of grave this man might have had. Defoe had a shadowy past: he worked as a spy for the English government, watching and reporting on Scottish issues. He occasionally fell foul of the law with his writings, ending up in the stocks for three days in 1703 at Charing Cross after writing a "seditious libel" entitled *The Shortest Way with Dissenters*. It was a satirical piece suggesting that we shouldn't impose laws on religious dissenters, we should kill them! It would cost him three days in the pillory with all manner of filth being thrown at him, dirt and rotten eggs, but his three days were a light punishment compared to many martyrs before him who had had their ears cut off in punishment for similar crimes.

He wrote many pieces of work, over five hundred titles, from poetry to religious pamphlets, as well as his novels, which included *Robinson Crusoe* in 1719, followed in the same year by *The Further Adventures of Robinson Crusoe*. Probably the best known of his other titles is *Moll Flanders*, written in 1722.

He lived through the Great Fire of London, with his house one of just three in the area of Shoreditch that escaped the fire. He also witnessed the Plague, which took 700,000 lives in London. In his youth he saw the plague pits being dug for the thousands of bodies that had succumbed to the pestilence, writing about it in his book entitled *The Plague Years*. When in London 9,000 people a week were dying, "there was not enough living to bury the dead".

He supported the failed Monmouth rebellion in 1685 when the rebellious James Scott, Duke of Monmouth and "natural" son of Charles II, took up arms to supplant his uncle, King James II. Battle was joined at Sedgemoor where the rebels were totally defeated. The Duke of

Monmouth was beheaded near the Tower of London receiving six blows with the executioner's axe, and then a knife to remove his head!

Daniel Defoe was captured after the battle and eventually managed to receive a pardon for his part in it, albeit forfeiting a large fine and some land he owned. In 1688 he supported the new monarch William III and was employed as a spy under this regime. He died in London in 1731.

I entered the cemetery near Old Street called Bunhill Fields, but to find Daniel Defoe's body in the graveyard would take some doing, as there was nothing to state where exactly in the cemetery he lay. The graveyard was well groomed and very pleasant. Strange, huge, figlike trees overhung the cemetery in places and added to the ambience of the walk around. I saw a man tending the vegetation around the perimeter of the grass verge to the pathways around the area and thought it best to ask for directions to where Defoe might rest, this man obviously being the graveyard caretaker. I asked about Defoe's last resting place and the man replied, "You're standing on him: he's all around you, Jock!" His cockney smile did not impress me much, and I found the man to be laughing at my expense. I was about to mention that I'd just watched Scotland win one-nil at Wembley the previous week, to take the grin off his graveyard-like dentures, but thought better of it, deciding to walk away from the rude laughing gardener and continue my search.

After a while I came to a monolith, a monument of white stone, rising high above all else. It was the grave of Daniel Defoe, I had found it!

16 Daniel Defoe's obelisk in the Bunhill Fields cemetery

DANIEL DE-FOE
BORN 1661,
DIED 1731,
AUTHOR OF
ROBINSON CRUSOE

But the huge column wasn't Defoe's original gravestone. It even said on it that it had been put up in 1870, more than a century after Defoe's death and burial. So what happened to the original stone? Later I found out that his grave was struck by lightning and the stone had been moved to Stoke Newington Library. Then it was moved again to Hackney Museum.

They say lightning never hits the same place twice. Well, maybe it wasn't lightning exactly, but in 1941 Adolf Hitler's *Luftwaffe* dropped tonnes of bombs on London including the cemetery, demolishing a good chunk of it. And then that bit was redesigned and landscaped in the 1960s. So the gardener was probably right after all. Defoe was indeed "all around". I had indeed

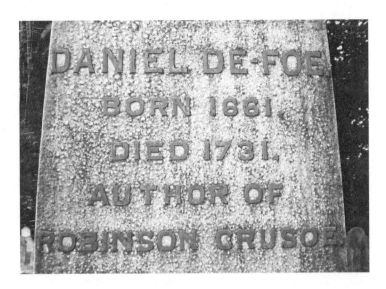

17 The words on Defoe's monument

been "standing on him" Wherever I was in the graveyard I was standing on him! You have to laugh!

With the authority of the church session putting the fear of death into Largo's inhabitants I found a great piece from the Kirk sessions May 1720 ...

> David Simpson summoned to appear before the Kirk session for behaving in an excited and improper manner, and using language which he ought not. He freely admitted that he had been swearing rather freely, and the Kirk session taking into consideration the fact that a day or two before his wife had presented him with twins. The session limited the censure to a private rebuke instead of a public one.

Another case at the Kirk sessions had John Edison in trouble for gathering sea wares on the beach on the Sabbath! He was seen lifting nets from the boats (e.g. working) 15 minutes into Sunday morning (12.15 a.m.) he exclaimed "he had no timepiece and was ignorant of the time". He was rebuked along with another man who had had the misfortune of falling asleep during the Sunday service!

Chapter 7

The Madness of Andrew Mason

Today being March 15, the Scottish newspapers have a photo of me plastered all over them. It's the sixteenth time this year, and you may well ask why. In the town of Pittenweem in Fife, the location of my first book *The Weem Witch*, a debate is at long last taking place on the subject of raising a memorial to the witches in my book. The 26 people who suffered the fate of the inquisition here deserve a reminder of what they suffered, and I am arguing for the motion to take reality.

It has taken me six years to get this far and if it happens it will be a first in Britain, a monument put up by the authorities for the atrocious acts carried out by the churches.

There is a monument in Torsåker in Sweden where seventy-one people, mostly children, were beheaded in one day, then burnt in a huge fire. Furthermore, there is one in Salem, Massachusetts, where twenty-one people were hanged for witchcraft. These two areas are huge tourist attractions and many films and books have been produced on the terrible acts that were committed here. Arthur Miller wrote a play inspured by the Salem witches called *The Crucible*. It has influenced about thirty other books and one major film starring Winona Rider and Daniel Day-Lewis. The Pittenweem ministry killed eighteen people as witches, and tortured many more and it is high time they too had a monument to them here, but there are many who oppose this, preferring the past to be forgotten.

The argument is set, and better people than me may carry the flag in future. One question put to me was: "What about all the people related to the ministers and council that killed the witches here? Would they not feel persecuted and angry that their names are now blackened by what their relations have done in the past? Would the monument not embarrass them and put them in a bad light today?"

Now there's a good question! Look at me! Leonard Low, forty-five, middle-aged, two kids, mortgage, no criminal record. I donate to several charities, am quite a kind person and hardworking ... but I also have my ancestors.

One was a madman who killed 348 people! His name was Captain Andrew Mason.

Andrew Mason was born in Largo, in an area called Largo Ward. Of his early life little is known, but he was one of eleven children. Infant mortality was high in the early 19th century, and the family records we have on him show he was one of two boys called Andrew born to the Mason family — his older brother Andrew died young.

Like a lot of Largo people before him, he found the magnetic lure of the sea too powerful to resist. His fame, like Sir Andrew Wood's and Alexander Selkirk's, would begin on board a ship as captain. His ship's name was the *Annie Jane*.

The *Annie Jane* was a Canadian boat, built in Quebec in 1853, and registered in Liverpool. Owned by a company called Holderness and Chilton, she was 1,294 tonnes, 55 metres long and 10 metres wide. She was classified as a brig, with two main masts rigged for square sails. Brigs were popular ships as they could be handled with a smaller crew than the heavier tea clipper ships.

It was to be her maiden voyage, taking a heavy cargo of iron railway tracks and barrels of beef and pork to Quebec. There was a large number of passengers to come aboard, with many being tradesmen enlisted for the building of the Canadian railroads. Others were Irish and Scottish immigrants together with their large families. On board they were shoehorned into cramped living spaces. Fourteen cubic feet (about 0.4 cubic metres) were allocated per person, but the captain had pushed in more than that allowed, so as to make the first journey of this ship as profitable as possible for the Canadian owners.

The journey to Canada would normally take forty days, and there was an accepted average mortality rate of 1 in 10 amongst the passengers. For example, in November 1853, 13,762 people sailed from Europe to America in 28 ships, and 1,141 people would not reach the shorelines of the USA, being dropped into the sea, dead from a multitude of diseases during the voyage.

On 23 August 1853 the *Annie Jane* was berthed at Liverpool, and after loading her provisions, cargo and crew, she was set for the 40-day journey to Canada. More than 415 passengers had been squeezed aboard. This number was the paying adults; whole families were on board, as emigration to Canada was the intention of many passengers, so at a modest estimate we could probably add another fifty or so children. Then add the crew!

Overall it's a picture of a miserable existence aboard a ship crammed full of desperate people wanting to start life afresh on another continent. What the conditions were like below can only be imagined, as children cried and adults fought each other for the most meagre of spaces on board.

A writer can envisage a picture to entertain his reader, and sometimes adding artistic licence can elaborate a scene setting, exaggerating the factual events to enhance a dramatic read. With the coming events of the *Annie Jane* disaster and her mad Captain Mason, my best option is to refer to a newspaper's examination of the disaster as printed later in the *Adelaide Advertiser* and I quote it in full.

A NOTABLE SHIPWRECK

Loss of the *Annie Jane*

FOUR HUNDRED SOULS PERISH

The greatest sea tragedy on the long list of Scottish shipwrecks was enacted in September 1853 on the bleak and treacherous Island of Vatersay, Barra, now the property of the state, and until a couple of years ago the theatre of which was fought one of the keenest conflicts in the struggle of land reforms in the Hebrides.

The grim drama of the wreck of the emigrant ship *Annie Jane*, culminating in the treacherous tableau of the total destruction of the ship and of the death of four hundred persons, is of the most thrilling description. The ill-starred ship, which sailed from Liverpool on August 23 with 415 emigrants, exclusive of infants, was owned by Messrs. Holderness and Chilton, and was commanded by Captain Mason. The emigrants were Scotch and Irish, and the former included one hundred Glasgow carpenters proceeding to Canada, then setting out upon its career of expansion and development. The *Annie Jane* left Liverpool under the most promising auspices. But she had only been two days at sea when the good fates forsook her for the furies, which dogged her until she disappeared beneath the waves. Evil omens came fast and faster. On the night of August 25th she encountered heavy gales, and because of the deficient stowage of her cargo she rolled so heavily to windward that she carried away her fore and mizzen topmasts. At the earnest solicitations of the passengers the Captain unwillingly put back to Liverpool.

She sailed again on September 9th and on the 12th met another terrific gale, which carried away her fore and mizzen topmasts and lower mastheads. When this happened the jib boom had to be cut away to clear the ship of the wreck. She lay to for a couple of days and the crew rigged up a jury foreyard, upon which the sail was set. There was now great and palpable danger, and the captain was again earnestly solicited to put back to Liverpool. He reluctantly consented, but when night came down he put the ship about for Quebec.

The following morning, when it became known that the captain had broken his word, there was the utmost consternation, because in her battered and hopeless condition, everybody knew the *Annie Jane* would never cross the Atlantic. When they remonstrated with him he boldly declared:— "I'm the master of this ship, it's Quebec or the bottom, and a bullet for the man who dares to interfere with me in my duty." From the evening of the 21st to the night of the 28th the ship drifted hopelessly and helplessly, when the wind again rose to a furious gale, the tumultuous sea rolling mountains high! Fear began to fall on the emigrants — the fear of death — and the feeling was intensified by the horrible darkness that seemed to grow deeper and blacker. The passengers realised that they were on the brink of a dire catastrophe, that the ship was hanging on the verge of death.

The captain foresaw the panic that was taking possession of the emigrants; he also may have foreseen that his foolhardiness might, in the final life-and-death grapple that was now imminent, involve him in a death much more painful than that which the greedy sea might inflict upon him, and he gave orders to clear the decks. When he got every passenger underneath, he fastened the hatches, and held the situation. Out of the black darkness surrounding him there loomed up, weird and ghostly, the outlines of a mountain. He had no notion what the place was in which the ship was drifting — all that he knew was that the *Annie Jane* was doomed. That no power on earth could save her now.

It was past midnight and the storm roared and screamed. He kept his ship towards the mountain — on through the darkness she moved, like something human, to her death. There is a grating sound as she takes the ground. At last the death blow has come. There was a quivering crash and an ominous shudder. The passengers knew that the end had come. In that final awful struggle where Death was king the fastened hatches gave quickly away in the clutches of those who were face to face with the unknown.

One of the survivors who escaped by a skylight from this house of death said:— "When the ship grounded I was in the cabin, which filled instantly with water, drowning the majority of the passengers there, and whose dead bodies completely blocked up the companionway. Scores of men, women and children were drowned or trampled to death."

The deck was soon black with figures — dim shadowy figures, who shouted in the delirium of madness when they realised the ship had come to her utmost bearings, and was steadily settling down.

When the first shock was over the emigrants rushed to the boats, three of which were placed between the mizzenmast and the poop, and the fourth on the top of the gang-house forward. When they got to the boats they found they were all fixed down and secured or lay bottom up.

Words are powerless to describe the agonising scenes which followed upon this discovery — the last spark of hope was rudely extinguished, and grim despair alone remained; but as they stood clustering round the boats they had not long to wait. A tremendous sea smote with a voice of thunder the quivering vessel. She staggered and reeled for a moment, and the ponderous bulk then broke into three pieces, carrying with her into the wild trough of the sea scores of human beings. All the survivors were clinging to the poop with the exception of seven men, who had fastened themselves to what remained of the topgallant mast. The poop fortunately floated and drifted inwards, and finally grounded about 4 o' clock in the morning. About the same time the seven men on the mast reached the shore.

A mile from the scene of the wreck was the farm steading of the Vatersay, and the labourers there upon hearing the cries for help hastened to the spot. With the aid of these men the remains of the mizzenmast, which were still attached by the shrouds to the wreck of the poop, were formed into a sort of bridge or ladder between the poop and shallow water, and by means of this the survivors were all got ashore by 7 in the morning.

When mustered they numbered 102, one of whom was a child, 12 women, and 28 of the crew, exclusive of the captain, who was also saved. The wild bleak shore upon which the survivors found themselves was literally black with the dead bodies of their friends and relatives. It was estimated there was a total loss of life of 400. Almost all the cabin passengers perished, including Captain Rose, of Quebec, and his wife. Only one child was saved, that of an Irish woman, who with her two children was going to America to join her husband. Her brave struggle to save her own life and that of her children is told at many a fireside in the long winter evenings in the island of Barra to this day — how she bound one child upon her back with her poor tartan shawl and grasped the other in her arms — how she held them fast until the cruel breakers in the last deadly assault, smashed the ship into pieces, and at the same time snatched from her motherly hold the little one that was pressed close to her bosom.

The ship smashed into rocks at latitude 56 57 N, longitude 7 35 W. There were fewer than fifty people living on the island, mainly as crofters and fishermen; they offered comfort and aid to the 102 survivors; some of the cargo of barrels of beef was washed up and opened so they could at least eat. The survivors were ...

Saved from the first class cabin (8 persons) Captain Mason – Francis Goold (surgeon) – Lammert Van Buren – Jane Francois Cornu – Marc Ami – John Morgan – Wm. Anfield (steward) – James Tailor (2nd steward)

Steerage passengers (61 survivors) Cath. Stanley – Bridget Sullivan – William Kelly – Mary Kelly – Amelia Kelly – Thomas McCarthy – John O'Brien – Julia McCarthy and child – Mary Sheridan – James Grogan – John Kingston – Mary Clifford – John Clifford – Alex. Walker – Thomas Kavanagh – James Kelly – Martha Marrah – Mary J. Getty – Cath. Burt – Mary J. Crothens – Jane Farrell – Thomas Hawkins – Edward Donnelly – Rosina Nohen – Patrick Kelly – Ellen Kelly – Timothy Donovan – Patrick Donnell – George Kingston – Patrick Shea – Alex. Allen – Mathew Toomey – George Lennox – Timothy Rogers – John Rogers

– James Rogers – John Brooks – Abraham Brooks – Charles Smith – Donnell Frazer – William Frazer – John Parry – David Caullen – Corney Mahony – John Townsley – James Admonson – William Reynolds – Robert Walter – Edward Shanehan – Alexander McCormic – Walter Fannier – Mathew Hayes – John Macnamara – Agnes Mattison – William Shack – Rachel Barry – Margaret McCauley – Martin Donough.

Crew survivors (33 sailors) Tom Markham (second mate) – William Lewis – William Moore – Tom Mason – Charles Lea – Tom Tillister – William Lancaster – Tom Nalcrow – Richard Stephens – Charles Burnock – James Sword – Christopher Kelly – Francis Welch – James Wood – Mathew Irwin – James Marshall – John Hutchinson – John Jackson – Charles Garret – James Allen – Edward Roberts – Charles Brown – Anthony Lizzard – Theordore Sherrett – Odu Simiez – Tom Berniez – Longlin Ward – Joe Dean – Joseph Miller – Archy Jameson – Edward Duray – Tom Gilbraith – James Boyd.

Total – 102 survivors.

The dead were buried in a communal pit just up from the beach.

There is today a stone memorial for the dead; it reads:

On 28th September 1853 the ship Annie Jane with emigrants from Liverpool to Quebec was totally wrecked in this bay and three fourths of the crew and passengers numbering about 350 men woman and children were drowned and their bodies interred here.

On the island there are no trees, so very little wood was available for coffins, but what wood could be found was used to make rough coffins for one of the ship's crew. This was for the first mate, a man called Bell. Another was made for a French Canadian Priest. The coffins were made from the timber wreckage from the ship.

Records of the named dead never survived the wreckage, so absolute was the sinking. It is estimated that 350 died in the crushed boat as it split into three; it is obvious to see by the report of the mangled remains that the cargo of iron railings for the railroads in Canada had broken loose, displaced or snapped the bonds that held the heavy weights in place. With the orders to batten hatches and stay below, when the railings broke free the tightly packed emigrants were crushed against the walls. With the water from the breech pouring in, the total confusion and darkness contributed to the helplessness they felt to the last. They never stood a chance on the lower decks, men, women and children.

The bodies from the wrecked *Annie Jane* washed ashore for three days afterwards.

During the First World War, in 1917, a British merchantman called the *Idomeneus* suffered a German torpedo exploding on board just off the island of Vatersay. In the accident three men were killed in the explosion, and the three bodies were put in the *Annie Jane* grave pit.

Reading the report from the surviving witnesses of the *Annie Jane* disaster, we see that the ship when hitting the rocks breaks itself into three parts. Just before this event one of the hatches blows off and the lower deck is instantly flooded, killing the terrified passengers below very quickly. From the men who searched and then buried the bodies

18 The beach on Vatersay Island where Captain Mason and the survivors made it to land. The *Annie Jane* hit the rocks to the right of the picture; for three days the 350 bodies of the passengers were washed on to the beach here.

that washed up on the shore over the next three days, came reports that they showed terrible crushing wounds. Myself and the reader can only guess what happened, but I am lucky enough to know a man who for thirty years has worked at sea in the British merchant navy. Tying down huge loads was a daily occurrence for this man. His reputation for tight, no-nonsense, thorough procedure on trips to the Middle East and Japan (to give a couple of examples) led to him being promoted to First Deck Officer on board the ships of a British firm — the Ben Line company.

His name is Donald Low, my older brother, and this old sea dog can tell from the reports of the wreck exactly what happened inside the *Annie Jane* to cause so much damage. He also has been to Vatersay island himself to see where our ancestor Captain Mason caused so much havoc and misery, on that lonesome, sandy beach in the Western Isles.

His words follow ...

"The *Annie Jane*, like all wooden ships before her, had a working life of around 20 years' service. Rot of the timbers and general wastage would take its toll before the inevitable would happen; if the company could afford it, a complete overhaul of the worn-out ship could be done, but with the expense of this it could be easier to just scrap the old one and buy a new ship. The other possibility was to sell the ship off for a buyer to use it for nothing but light domestic sailing. The timbers would last till nature claimed them. [as with Alexander Selkirk on the *Cinque Ports*]

"The Brig class of ship were tough boats, specially designed for carrying heavy loads. From what I can make of the evidence given, the reasons for the disaster are fairly obvious to me.

"The cargo reported to be in the hold, is heavy iron railway lines, sheet metal, barrels of pork and beef. The cargo itself is a very heavy weight, so it wouldn't take a lot of the cargo to produce the standard safe weight the boat was designed for carrying. Knowing the mind of Captain Mason on his first voyage for the company, he was sure to want to impress his bosses at Holderness and Chilton and make sure they got a handsome return, so overloading the bulk of the precious cargo was a certainty.

"The cargo being heavy it made up quickly the weight the ship was designed to carry; with so little room taken up they could fill the remaining space on board with emigrant passengers. A painted line would be on the outside of the boat showing the draught to the sea line with regards to overloading the ship, basically the safe line.

"The cargo was wedged down tight with timber. Wedges of timber would be positioned against the ship's hull walls to the cargo, wedging everything tight and tied down with ropes.

"Everything in the hold would have been brought aboard by releasing one of the many hatches the ship had. I would expect the *Annie Jane* to have had a cargo access hatch maybe 8ft wide. It could be fastened into place by poles holding the hatches in place. With the report on the flooding quickly drowning the passengers, it is fairly certain the hatch was first to give way, probably hitting the rocks full on, the infill of water from the 8-foot hatch would have flooded the hold in a matter of seconds. With the additional weight of water on board, the ship's stability would be shot to bits. With the weight all below the ship, the nautical term is 'the boat's still': it would give a whiplash effect to the mast and sails toiling in what were reported as 100-foot waves on the night of the storm. The masts would snap with the shock as the boat rocked in the waves hitting her. The water pouring inwards would have destroyed the wedges, with the 500 passengers being battered against them. And with the wedges gone the iron railings and barrels would have come loose, to smash and crush the people crammed inside the hold. They had no hope in there as Captain Mason had ordered the deck access doors to be shut, total carnage. The movement of the metal cargo and the fierceness of the storm dumping the ship on the rocks would be enough for the total destruction of the boat.

"I visited the island in 2011 and locals told me there was still a large metal boiler along one of the beaches, the last bit of wreckage from the *Annie Jane*. Steam power was in its infancy but it may have been used to pull the sails."

"Donald Low"

Captain Mason, in his desperation to impress his ship's new owners, had set sail twice in a horrific storm, and twice limped back to harbour, running up costs for critical repairs. His third attempt, after brandishing a pistol at anyone in his crew who would disagree with his command, set things in motion for all-out disaster. His bloody-mindedness where others warned of caution, cost the lives of around 350 people. The advice from others in Liverpool harbour to sit out the storm was ignored. With nothing but pride and money on his mind, they sailed off on the orders of Captain Mason into oblivion.

As I said, I'm related to this man, on my mother's side of the family. Andrew's father, also called Andrew, was born in 1770: he married Agness Cunningham, also born in 1770, in Kemback church in Fife. They had fourteen children, the first born in St Andrews, all the others born in Largo, names as follows.

1. John Berwick Mason, born	4.2.1798
2. Andrew Mason	17.4.1800...died young
3. Euphemia Mason	15.7.1802
4. David Mason	8.7.1804
5. Jean Mason	30.11.1806
6. Thomas Mason	−.6.1809
7. Grizel Mason	19.8.1810
8. ANDREW MASON	5.7.1812
9. Robert Mason	2.10.1814
10. Peter Webster Mason	2.10.1814
11. Janet Goodsir Mason	−.−.1816
12. Archibald Goodsir Mason	8.7.1816
13. Anstruther Mason	24.1.1819
14. James Durham Mason	24.1.1819

After all that Agness Mason deserves a mighty good rest, having been continually pregnant for the best part of twenty years, and giving birth to two sets of twins amongst them! It's interesting to see the twins Janet Mason and Archibald (1816) being given middle names of "Goodsir".

The next chapter is dedicated to the Goodsir family, who originated in Largo from a well-loved man who was the area's doctor. He did his rounds by horse, starting off on a Monday and returning to his house on Friday. He was an eccentric man with a large family himself. It looks like the twins may have been given their middle name from the doctor who delivered them!

My own family tree stems from the last of Agnes's children, James Durham Mason.

Chapter 8

Not So Good Sir!

In the course of reading many books that tell of the dignified, notable and esteemed men of Fife, the name Dr John Goodsir of Largo keeps coming to my attention. He was born in Wemyss in 1746, the year of the Battle of Culloden, when Jacobite dreams to recapture the throne of Britain were cruelly ended. The doctor seemed a very colourful individual to all in his practice in the Lands of Largo, and admiration from his patients and colleagues give him a fantastic pedigree. He's noted as being a "large-nosed tall wiry giant of a man, aye ready with mull (snuff)" who rode his rounds on a horse. He used to fill his saddlebags with supplies on a Monday and travel through Largo on his horse and be back home on the Friday, staying overnight as a guest in many of the houses he came to as their doctor. He tied lamps to his knees so he could see where he was going at night as he travelled the country, to the great mirth of his patients who could see him coming in the far distance, "travelling to gather modest fees at distances far from his own door". Such a beloved man was lamented after his death by his patients as "his piety became as noted as his physic". He married a Largo girl,

Agness Johnstone and had eleven children; three of these would become surgeons themselves. One of these surgeons, also named John, moved to Anstruther, where when he grew up he would have a practice to rival his father. He in turn would have six children in Anstruther of whom three would become sickly and die. Two sons John (born 1814) and Harry would take on the family business, and continue with a tradition that had all started with their grandfather in Largo.

It is here with the two sons where I find the darker side in Dr John and sadly and most horribly in the story of Dr Harry Goodsir. I suppose the reader may now accuse me of cheating as both these men were born outside Largo's borders, and yes, you may have a point, but their father and grandfather were both born within the Largo parish boundary, and the two of them would certainly mould John and Harry into the professions learnt from their elders in Largo. Both would have titles of distinction for their trade; but one would end his life in the most agonisingly torturous way in a bleak wasteland of the Arctic, using the tools of his trade to produce a most disgusting spectacle, a subject most vilified and heinous, so far not covered in the pages of Largo's history ... the act of cannibalism!

John and Harry were schooled in Anstruther, then at St Andrews University, qualifying as a pathologist and morphologist (morphology is the biological study of organisms). So keen were they in their studies, that the brothers converted the house in Anstruther to have a special laboratory for their research. Writing in 1886, D. Hay Fleming wrote of this abode: "The upper room of the house formed a wing of the main building, in order that they could not be interrupted during experiments by idle or inconvenient curiosity, the regular entrance to the home was barricaded shut. The room above where the brothers worked was only reachable by an elaborate trap door system."

The nature of what was going on in this secret room is fairly obvious. Their chosen field would require dissection, but dissection needed fresh bodies! At this time in the early 19th century, pathology was one of the leading sciences of the day. The demand for fresh corpses put a strain on the universities. They couldn't get enough, because only the bodies of those condemned to death in the courts could be offered to the surgeons to practise on. A prisoner condemned in the courts would be hanged, but if universities relied on this route of hanged cadavers, they might only get one body a year to dissect.

With an almost unlimited demand for bodies coming from doctors and scientists, who would certainly turn a blind eye to the source of any fresh cadaver that was put their way, an underground trade in body-snatching arose. Grave robbing became rife and was paid handsomely!

The famous body-snatchers of Edinburgh, William Burke and William Hare, used to guess the position of the corpse, looking for the head end of the coffin. They would dig down to it and smash the end open, then insert two hooks to go under the arms of the cadaver, and pull the body out the coffin with ropes. This could be done leaving little trace of what had taken place.

But after a while they found raiding graves to be far too much like hard work, so decided that instead of doing all the digging, and risking being caught pulling bodies from the graveyards, they would murder selected victims instead as an easier way to get bodies. A surgeon called

Doctor Robert Knox at Edinburgh University would pay upwards of £7/10/- for a fresh corpse: that's over £700 in our money today! They murdered seventeen times, bringing people back to their house in Edinburgh, where they would get the unfortunate guests very drunk, then strangle them or suffocate them with a pillow. Robert Knox was happy to accept the bodies and no questions whatsoever were asked, until they were caught, that is!

One corpse they offered Dr Knox was that of a local lad, who used to walk the streets with a leg deformity. He was called "daft Jamie" by all who knew him, and when his body turned up on the dissecting table, he was instantly recognised. Some had seen the lad only days earlier, looking well and healthy. Questions were raised, police were called. Dr Knox had to tell the police where the bodies in his university had come from, and Burke and Hare were soon arrested at the house they shared.

Inside the house, under a bed, the police found another body killed just hours earlier, ready to be taken over to the university. To save himself from the hangman's rope, Hare turned "King's Evidence", telling all about their murderous trade, and the numbers killed. (Turning King's evidence would have you released from all blame of a crime you had committed, but your evidence would condemn others involved in the crime.)

The bodies would be eagerly dissected in front of up to a hundred paying students; two of these students at the time of Dr Knox's lectures were John and Harry Goodsir. It seems fairly obvious to me that the careful preparations taken at the house in Anstruther were for their own secret dissections. In all probability they were receiving bodies themselves from the graveyard, which just happens to be just across the road from their house.

The story of the body-snatchers in Edinburgh has been made into several books and films; I won't go into further details on the case but William Burke was publicly hanged for his crimes, with his accomplice William Hare giving King's Evidence and being set free.

Burke's body, funnily enough, would go to the dissecting chamber after his hanging and was possibly observed by the Goodsir brothers themselves. (An American surgeon commented on one of Knox's lectures: "the sights were extremely disagreeable, many of them shocking beyond all I ever thought could be. I was glad to leave this charnel house and breath the fresh air again")

William Burke's skeleton and death mask can be viewed today at the Anatomy Museum in Edinburgh.

The house the Goodsir brothers had in Anstruther for their studies was abandoned, when Edinburgh became their home. They settled there and received a licence from Royal Edinburgh's college of surgeons and one of the brothers became curator of the university's anatomical museum. But the new owners of the Anstruther house said "the compartment up high in the house continued to bear many a trace of the dissecting room" — one can read a thousand thoughts from this statement, again taken from D. Hay Fleming.

In 1845 Harry was chosen for a special voyage by an illustrious Arctic explorer. Sir John Franklin needed a naturalist and surgeon on board one of his two new steamships the *Erebus* and *Terror*. The planned voyage was to explore the possibilities for a breakthrough via the fabled North West passage through the Arctic, with the destination being a route to China via the icy wastes of the North Pole. To trade with China involved a two-year voyage around the coast of Africa, but finding a passage to the North, through the pack ice and uncharted coastline of the Arctic, could in theory reduce the journey by half. At a time when Britain had no significant overseas enemies, but a massive naval force (the navy had just fought Napoleon and the Spanish), sections of the shipping fleet were sent on voyages of exploration. It was a time when the source of the River Nile was found, Africa was being explored by those such as David Livingstone and Mungo Park, and many ships already had been sent north to map out the Arctic. But so far all had had severe difficulty, some staying for two years stuck in the ice. The summer was short but during it water inlets were free of ice; however when winter descended the ships became trapped in metres-thick ice.

The hope was to find an inlet that would allow ships to sail through the polar area and out the other side towards China. The two ships HMS *Erebus* (372 tonnes) and HMS *Terror* (326 tonnes), had steam power which was basically a new invention in ships. They also had copper plates bolted around the base of the ship to strengthen the hull so that it could smash through the thick ice. The new screw propeller was fitted and for the first time ever the boats were centrally heated by pipes from the engine. Never before had a voyage been so well prepared: tinned food was stored aboard, again a new invention in its infancy. They had the best science officers aboard and the most experienced Arctic captain available in Sir John Franklin.

No one expected anything but success from the two ships as they sailed down the Thames. London newspapers had been carrying the story for weeks and expectations were high as they left to a massive send-off, people lining both sides of the river to see the famous captain ... but not one of the 129 crew on both ships would be seen alive again.

Doctor Harry Goodsir was on the *Erebus* as acting surgeon and the voyage left the Thames on 19 May 1845.

The next stop would be the Orkney Islands then on to the Arctic Circle. The two boats carried 2,075 kilograms of lemon juice in large kegs to protect against scurvy, 15,664 tins of meat, 10,452 tins of soup, 3,555 kilograms of tinned vegetables and 1,185 kilograms of tinned potatoes.

Overall there were supplies for a three-year voyage; the Admiralty expected them to be stuck in pack ice for at least one winter, and they were advised to deposit food on the ice for future trips. The canned food contract had been won by an East End businessman called Goldner: it was a lucrative contract, but was delivered late, with one day to spare before sailing. Because it was so late, no one had the chance to check or taste the food. This was to be a key cause of the whole disaster of the voyage.

The boats next stopped at Greenland and letters were taken and sent to loved ones back in Britain, Harry Goodsir writes in a letter to his brother with great excitement: "June 28th a dredge was sunk to a depth of 300 fathoms [about 550 metres] and living animals were brought up".

The ships were last seen on the 26th of July entering Lancaster Sound which was the gateway into the frozen wastes of the Arctic. This is the last time the ships were seen by Europeans.

The ships were carrying enough food for three years but by 1848 the Admiralty was starting to get worried, as

19 Harry Goodsir photographed just before the Arctic voyage in 1845

no word of the expedition had surfaced in all the time they had been at sea. Copper casings in which messages were to be deposited in the sea at intervals of every few days, to float in the tide and be picked up by other sailors, had never been found.

Under pressure from open pleas by Sir John Franklin's wife for the Admiralty to do more, they offered a £20,000 reward for any ship that would assist in the search and recovery of the crews of the *Erebus* and *Terror*.

Within a few months, ship after ship would be heading north to the Arctic to join the search for Franklin. The romance of it all caught the public eye with the newspapers eagerly printing details on every ship and captain leaving the harbours. Heroic captains and friends of Sir John boarded what ice-worthy vessels were available and headed north. Harry's brother was one such person. For six years nothing was found, and some of the rescue ships had actually fallen into difficulty themselves.

HMS *Investigator*, all 422 tonnes of her, was last seen stuck in the ice in 1854. She vanished later in an area called Mercy Bay on Beechy Island in Canada's North West Territory. (She has recently been found sitting 10 metres under the water by a Canadian team of archaeologists working for Parks Canada.)

But, gradually, fragmented information about the Franklin expedition began to be found, and a horrible, horrible story began to unfold.

Three graves were found in 1854: they were men from the crews of both ships, and they had used wooden boards as grave markers. The grave site had been found very near the area where the HMS *Investigator* had come into difficulty and became grounded in the ice. The boards marking the graves gave the names of...

John Torrington died Jan 1st 1846
John Hartnell died Jan 5th 1846
William Braine died April 5th 1846

From this it appeared that John Hartnell and William Braine had died only seven months into the expedition! Both had served on Dr Harry Goodsir's ship, the *Erebus*. John Torrington had served on the *Terror*.

More information came when a stone cairn was found on King William Island, inside which was a copper tube holding a message dated 28 May 1847 which said that the two ships *Erebus* and *Terror* had wintered at Beechy Island in 1845–46, then managed to drift in the ice to King William Island the next year, and all was well. It was written by Captain Crozier and said Sir John Franklin was leading the expedition.

But the note had been dug out of the cairn several weeks later, and rewritten. The amended note said that Sir John Franklin had died on 11 June 1847 and that nine other officers and fifteen men had died since. They planned to abandon the stricken ships and march by foot towards the Back River (on the Canadian mainland). Again it was signed by Captain Crozier. In a matter of a few weeks after writing that "all was well", 24 officers and crew had died, including the leader of the expedition.

What a disaster and high loss of life among the officers! What on earth could have gone wrong? With land rescue parties from America and Canada now working their way on foot, and at least 25 seaborne expeditions over the years, looking for any evidence of Sir John Franklin's party, it wasn't long before more evidence was found. In 1857 Captain Francis Leopold McClintock, a Royal Naval officer, was on his third effort to unravel the mystery of the crews of the *Terror* and *Erebus*, when one of his crew members made a significant find: a lifeboat lying on runners like skis, sitting in the ice-covered wastes, hidden in the deep snow. It was from the Franklin ships. It was obvious how desperate things had become for the crews, as they had been pulling the boat by ropes harnessed around the men. Inside were two skeletons, one with its head missing (taken by polar bears or wolves). Inside the boat was a clutter of goods — soap, cutlery, books, a heavy amount of chocolate and unopened tins of food with the Goldner stamp on them. Here was a vision of desperation and calamity. They couldn't have starved to death, judging from the food stored in the boat.

But to Captain McClintock, who guessed that the boat with its cargo was about 635 kilograms in weight, which would exhaust men pulling it in no time, the amount of unnecessary weight on board the boat being pulled by the men was very puzzling.

At King William Island, McClintock's party found evidence of a camp, and sporadic pieces of human bone were found sticking through the snow. A complete skeleton was found, lying face down, and there was a large flat stone nearby suggesting that the man stopped exhausted, maybe sat resting awhile, then rose to continue the walk, but was so weakened that he collapsed face down in the snow, to rise no more. Because the body had a gold tooth and wore part of an officer's uniform, they identified the body as one of the officers, Lieutenant Henry Le

Vesconte of the *Erebus*, as he was remembered to have had a gold cap on his teeth. The complete skeleton was first taken to America, then transported to the United Kingdom, where it was taken to Greenwich Hospital.

Another rescue party, this time from America, found more of Sir John Franklin's crew in 1879, again at King William Island where McClintock had found his decayed skeleton. Lieutenant Fredrick Schwatka found another body in a shallow grave, but this time it could be identified as Lieutenant John Irving from HMS *Terror*, as he had a sports medal around his neck (he was from Edinburgh). More staggering was the information Schwatka received from the Inuit tribesmen who fished here: they recalled meeting around forty white men walking with mouths of blood, in a single line through the snow, men dropping one by one. The tribesmen sold two seals to the men and watched as they walked away to oblivion in the fierce −45°C harshness of the landscape of rock and snow.

A sad picture now began to unfold, but was still not fully understood. Where bodies were found, huge piles of canned food were also found, still unopened, so starvation couldn't have been a factor. Scurvy was a problem experienced in previous expeditions, but the ships had plenty of lemon juice in many barrels on board which would counteract the ravishes of scurvy.

By a cove not far north of where they found Lieutenant John Irving's body, was found the final camp of Sir John Franklin's two crews. Over forty skulls were counted lying all around small fires. The tripod camp pots were still in position holding the last meals the crew had eaten ... in them were the unmistakable sight of human bones with saw-marks on them.

The remnants of Sir John Franklin's crews from the two ships had broken the final taboo ... cannibalism. The scattered bones all around the camp showed saw-marks where the meat had been whittled off and eaten. It was a pathetic glimpse of a once proud crew that had been given all the most modern technology available, of the most well prepared voyage ever to be undertaken, using the most experienced Arctic explorers that were available to the Admiralty. In the end, it had been a massive failure. The ships were deserted after two years stuck in the frozen seas and were probably crushed over time in the ice. A disaster had overcome them, with twenty-four dying in a short time. Panic and desperation having overcome the crew, they set out towards the Great Fish River (or Back River), which was within the boundaries of the Hudson Bay Company, hoping an outpost would be near enough for them to reach. But the boat on runners that had been found was pointing away from the river. It looked like they had given up on the long haul with the boat and tried to return to the ships, but exhaustion and cold had taken their toll on the party.

It could be that the ships broke into two parties, one pulling the boat for the Great Fish River, the other, amounting to about forty men, walking to King William Island to try to sight a rescue boat approaching. Whatever the plans were for both teams, it all ended in disaster.

A terrible story for sure, but what happened to Dr Harry Goodsir? What happened to the crew that killed so many officers and men? And why, with so many unopened tins of food, turn to cannibalism?

In August 1984, a Canadian anthropologist called Owen Beattie led a team of like-minded fellow scientists to

King William Island, with the intention of digging up the three graves that had been found there in 1854 and examining them thoroughly. The bodies were buried in the ice, so to bring them out they used heated water, a long process but there was really no other way to reach them without damaging the frozen body.

John Torrington's grave was first; he was found in a carefully prepared wooden coffin. His body was resting on a bed of wood shavings. They poured a constant stream of warm water into the coffin and once the ice had been melted away, over twenty-four hours, they found his body to be as freshly preserved as on the day he had died. He was 1.63 metres in height and was terribly underweight, weighing only 40 kilos. His job on board the *Erebus* was that of a stoker working below deck throwing spadefuls of coal into the steam burners of the ship all day. A man with that job could be expected to have hands with calluses and rough skin. But on the dissecting table his body was puny, his hands were smooth and his nails clean and tidy. It was obvious that he had not worked for many weeks, and had perhaps been bedridden with an illness of some sort.

No food was found in his digestive tract or stomach; his lungs were found to be blackened but this was to be expected in a man who had shovelled coal in a confined space. Samples of his hair and other tissues from his body were taken for further tests, and it was these tests that would finally answer why the expedition failed in the mysterious way it did. When the test results were examined in the laboratories, John Torrington showed a massive reading on lead content in his body.

A normal body may show a lead content of 5 to 14 parts per million of lead. But John Torrington showed 110 to 151 parts per million of lead, and a hair sample showed 600 parts per million! This would be enough to make the person affected feel dissipated, as though he had flu. In fact he would be seriously ill, with a wasting disease that would weaken the body slowly until pneumonia set in. It was a fatal scenario. But where had the lead come from? The clues were all around: where dead bodies had been found all around King William Island and by the dragged lifeboat, tins of unopened food were conspicuous everywhere, lying beside the skeletons. The Goldner-branded tins lay unopened, and the survivors had cannibalised their dead shipmates. The tins were tested by the scientists and were found to have lead solder seals on the lids and sides. The solder seals were shoddily made and had bled into the food inside, contaminating the contents. The tinned food was poisoned! In Goldner's rush to fulfil the huge, lucrative order, corners had been cut to get the consignment to the ships on time. With just one day's leeway before sailing, no tasting was done. The moment the crew stocked the food below in the ships' holds they were doomed!

But what happened to Dr Harry Goodsir, you may ask. Where was his body? A clue to his whereabouts came when the body of Lieutenant Henry Le Vesconte was taken to London's Greewich Hospital in 2011. Human skeletal biologist Simon Mays did a chemical analysis of the skeleton's teeth, using a technique that measures the concentration of strontium and oxygen levels in the bone, and matches them to the water supply of the region they lived in. They found the water supply had not come from Devon, where Lieutenant Vesconte had come from, but from Northern Britain, Scotland to be more precise. This skeleton definitely did not belong to Lieutenant Vesconte.

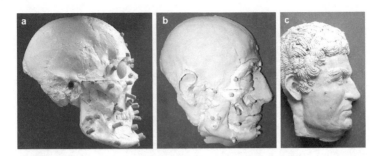

20 Building up from the skull — the process of reconstructing what turned out to be Goodsir's face

There was only one other officer on board with a gold tooth and of a similar age to Vesconte, and that was Dr Harry Goodsir — from Scotland. The researchers carried out a facial reconstruction with clay on the skull (using the same process as Dundee University has used on the Lundin Links Pictish skull). Once fleshed out with clay, it shows a remarkable likeness to a photograph of Dr Harry Goodsir taken just before the ships left London. With a degree of certainty, Simon Mays' team had identified the skeleton of Dr Harry Goodsir.

When the body of John Hartnel was exhumed by same the heated water method as John Torrington, it came as a great surprise to the scientists there to find that the body had already been autopsied — way back in 1846. The autopsy must have been carried out by the surgeon on board John Hartnel's ship, who would have been none other than Dr Harry Goodsir!

These 21st-century scientists could now compare an autopsy from the early 19th century. They found the normal Y-incision autopsy of today, but upside down, with cuts coming either side of the leg and up from the sternum.

21 The clay reconstruction of Vesconte's skull becomes Dr Goodsir! The skull they thought was Lieutenant Vesconte was fleshed out in Greenwich ...

Now the full sorry picture of what happened to the crews of the *Erebus* and *Terror* can be positively worked out. The ships travelled up Lancaster Sound. In the freezing winter of 1845, the ice had held the ships and drifted them around to King William Island where another year had passed. By this time the solder had bled into the contents of

... When finished and put against the photo of Dr Goodsir, it's a remarkable match!

the food in the cans. The officers used to eat separately from the crew, and from their meals they ingested heavy doses of lead in the food. Lead is a cumulative poison. They had been ingesting it from day one in very small amounts but now the cans had aged and more lead was present in every meal. The officers fell very ill, over the weeks dying one by one.

Next the lowly crew members came down with this strange pestilence. It wouldn't take much to work out that the tinned food was contaminated in some way, but they would never identify the precise cause. (Some of the artefacts found on King William Island have been the empty food tins shaped into basic mugs to be used as drinking vessels. The mug's owner must have been unaware that he was poisoning himself with every mouthful he took!)

The ships seemed to be permanently trapped in the thick sea ice, the food was suspect, the crew was wasting and slowly dying. Efforts to escape to safety had to be made on foot, one party pulling a boat by ropes towards the nearest outpost of the Hudson Bay Company, the other trying for King William Island to seek help from the rescue ships.

The boat was put on runners and dragged towards the Great Fish River, but some days into the journey it became obvious to all that, in their weakened state, they were going to fail to reach their objective. Exhausted, men fell and died by the wayside as the boat slid on.

Whoever was now in charge, seeing the hopeless situation they were in, made the decision to turn the boat about and return to the ships. They reversed and tried to reach the ships, but they had lost too many men, those who still survived were too ill, and they failed. The last two members of the boat-sled crew crawled into the boat, pulled a cover over themselves and waited to die. The ships' logs have never been found, but more artefacts of the Franklin expedition are still being discovered even today. With modern technology, some day soon we can expect to find the two ships *Erebus* and *Terror* lying under the sea after having been crushed and ruined by the shifting polar ice.

Maybe — just maybe — in some watertight, lead box — there lie the diaries and logs of the captains of the two ships. If so, we may eventually know the minds of those who perished here in the most awful of circumstances.

The other party travelled on foot towards King William Island. A pathetic picture comes to mind of forty-plus men stumbling onwards through the snow, walking in a drawn-out line, scurvy and pneumonia ravaging the men, who were bleeding from the mouth and other orifices. One by one they fell, to lie still in the snow. Some survivors eventually found a cove which offered basic shelter from the wind, but for them no rescue would come. It was the end! In their starvation they turned to eat their comrades who had already died. Who better to do the butchery than a trained surgeon? The cut marks on the bones that have been found show an evident expertise. Dr Harry Goodsir's dissecting saws could have been used here. In his last hours, frostbitten, starving, wet through, with the effects of lead ingestion leaving him weak and disoriented, Goodsir wandered a few hundred yards from the cove and the other men. Finding a flat-ended stone, he sat on it, rested a while and then tried to rise. He fell forward, he lay still and his world went black! For him the pain and his suffering were now over.

Chapter 9

Today's Largo

On the sands of Largo Bay, ten metres west from the old swings (now gone), the grassland here displays sporadic bumps up to a metre high in places. What most people do not realise is that these are the remains of the Pictish burial ground and the female shrine to the Veniconi Picts who lived here. There's no plaque or anything to tell you what you're walking over. Having been quite a find for archaeology, it is so sad this has been forgotten about.

I hope that with this book, we can achieve something permanent for the tourists here, a plaque with at least a bit of history about what was found here and the layout of the graves. Of the Roman remains up past Lundie Tower, nothing remains bar the information given from the man who stumbled into the Roman kitchens: he described the bright yellow sandstone in the building of the walls. Up past the tower on the Ceres road you can still see this yellowish stone in the fields on the right.

Sir Andrew Wood's tower still stands and is good for a visit. It is just one of the four he built, but a pile of rubble lies where another tower stood, so you can imagine the layout of the castle. It was a huge place in its day. Again everything has deteriorated and a farm now works the land here. Sir Andrew's grave is in the floor of Largo church but hidden by rows of pews. A model of his ship (the yellow caravel) has pride of place, sitting in view. The church is locked on most days, so access is a problem.

The Pictish stone showing the elephant is incarcerated in its own metal cage at the front of the church on the left hand side as you leave. No details or plaques mention anything about the witches that were taken in Largo. These records are in St Andrews with parish and court records. Lamont wrote his diaries from Lundie Tower which still stands, and can be reached by taking a right from the exit to Ceres along the Leven road.

Alexander Selkirk has a large statue in Lower Largo, standing where his house once stood. There is a hotel not far from here with his fictional doppelgänger's name, the Crusoe Hotel. There is a small room attached with panels on the wall dictating his story on the island. It is very basic, but the hotel's Crusoe theme continues through the bar, and it is well worth a visit as the meals are good. Daniel Defoe has a large monument in the Bunhill graveyard in London, watch out for cheeky cockney gardeners!

Nothing exists of the house Captain Mason was born in. But Dr Goodsir's house still stands today, straight across from the sea access used by the yacht club at Lower Largo. It's called 'GOODSIR HOUSE' in capitals above the door. The owner was kind enough to show me around, not knowing herself where the house got its name from. When I enlightened her on tales of vivisection and cannibalism, with facial reconstructions thrown in for good measure, I'm not so sure she wanted to know. The house is big and has many rooms, that once had eleven of the Goodsir children running about. The house of Goodsir's son after he moved to Anstruther, near the cemetery, has a plaque above it.

Please visit this area of Largo — it's a hidden gem of a place. My book may help you with the eventful and sometimes unpleasant history that happened here.

But look around, the golden sands, the mighty hills to climb and the great pubs and hotels highlight the ambiance of the place today. It is much friendlier than during its darker days, and I am sure the hospitality of the area will bring you back to this mysterious wee place again and again.

Leonard Low
14 April 2013
Lundin Links

Sources

Helpful books contributing information were ...

General

Historical Antiquities of Fife, James W. Taylor, 1875.

Guide to the East Neuk of Fife, D. Hay Fleming 1869

The Handy-Book of the Fife Coast, Henry Farnie, 1880

History of the County of Fife, Vol 3, John M Leighton, 1840

County Folk Lore Vol VII, John E Simpkins, 1912

Chapter 1 — Bones

The Inscriptions of Pictland, Frances Carney Diack, 1944

Chapter 2 — The Largo Picts Fight Roman Occupation

Interesting Roman Antiquities Recently Discovered in Fife, asserting the site of the great battle fought betwixt Agricola and Galgacus, Andrew Small, 1823

Chapter 3 — The Pirate Sir Andrew Wood

The Key of the Forth, John Jack, 1858

The Bass Rock, Thomas McCrie et al., 1848.

Records of the Scottish Court of Admiralty

Letters and Papers, Foreign and Domestic, Henry VIII, Vol 1, edited by J. S. Brewer, 1920.

The Story of Leith, John Russell, 1922

The Yellow Frigate, James Grant, 1850

Chapter 4 — Witches

St Andrews in 1645–46, David Robert Kerr, 1895 (Plague, Bishops)

Malleus Maleficarum, Heinrich Krämer and Jacob Sprenger, 1489

Witchcraft and Second Sight in Scotland, John Gregorson Campbell, 1902

Scotland's Black Death, Karen Jillings 2007

The Witches of Fife, Stuart MacDonald, 2002

A Calendar of Witchcraft Cases in Scotland 1510–1727, George F. Black, 2003

Gazetteer of Scotland, vol I and II, Robert and William Chambers, 1844 (Largo, St Andrews)

Bygone Church Life in Scotland, edited by William Andrews, 1899

Chapter 5 — Lamont's Diary

The Chronicle of Fife; Being the Diary of John Lamont of Newton from 1649 to 1672, 1810

Chapter 6 — What Shall We Do with a Drunken Sailor?

St Andrews University holds the Kirk sessions from Largo church, in which the early records of Alexander Selkirk can be found.

A Journal of the Plague Year, Daniel Defoe, 1722

A Cruising Voyage Round the World, Captain Woodes Rogers, 1712

Woodes Rogers's Privateering Voyage of 1708–11, B. M. H. Rogers, in *The Mariner's Mirror*, Vol 19, Issue 2, 1933.

The Life and Adventures of Alexander Selkirk, John Howell, 1829

Largo Village Book, by Leonora Rintoul, 1932

Chapter 8 — Not So Good Sir!

Anstruther, or Illustrations of Scottish Burgh Life, George Gourlay, 1888.

Fifiana, Matthew Forster Connolly, 1869

Narrative of a Journey to the Shores of the Polar Sea, Sir John Franklin, 1823

Sir John Franklin's Last Arctic Expedition, Richard J. Cyriax, 1997

Frozen in Time, the Fate of the Franklin Expedition, Owen Beattie and John Geiger, 2004

Also by Leonard Low
from Steve Savage Publishers

The Weem Witch

'The most complete account yet of the suffering inflicted upon the unfortunate victims of the anti-witch hysteria which gripped local communities in the 17th and 18th centuries ... Leonard, who hails from Upper Largo, said he was driven to write the book by a desire to commemorate these forgotten scapegoats. And the remarkable stories he has uncovered are fascinating, enriched as they are by a dense assortment of facts and personal accounts which are as gripping as they are enlightening ... the political turmoil brought about by the Act of Union meant these scandals were forgotten. Until now!'

— *East Fife Mail*

'Leonard Low's relentless and brutal account leaves nothing to the imagination. With a self-confessed love of horror, Low has taken historical manu-scripts, listened to the local lore, unearthed the woeful truth and added a large dose of his own inventiveness to come up with a spell-binding story of ignorance, fear and a world gone mad.'

— *Dumfries and Galloway Standard*

ISBN 978-1-904246-19-0

Paperback. Illustrated. RRP £6.99

Available from bookshops or directly from the publisher.

For information on mail order terms, see our web-site (www.savagepublishers.com) or write to: Mail Order Dept., Steve Savage Publishers Ltd., The Old Truman Brewery, 91 Brick Lane, LONDON, E1 6QL.